THE MONEY SECRET

What they said about *The Heart of Success* . . .

'I would recommend CEOs to give a copy of this book to every manager in their company.'

Jim Wright, Vice-President of Human Resources,
SmithKline Beecham, R & D

'Before you read one more book on how to climb the corporate ladder read this: it will help you make sure the ladder is leaning against the right wall.'

Kevin Kaiser, Adjunct Professor of Finance, INSEAD and
Vice-President of Product Development at bfinance.com

'Rob Parsons has an uncanny ability for asking some of life's most challenging questions in an unobtrusive way. If you need to take time to reflect on who you are, what you value, and how you can live more of the life you believe in, then this book is a great place to start.'

Jill Garrett, Managing Director, The Gallup Organisation, UK

'This will be the most talked about business book of the year – it is essential reading for anybody who is concerned about genuine people and business development.'

Professor Jim Saker, Business School, Loughborough University

'Stress, burn-out and absenteeism due to illness are becoming the hallmarks of some companies. That's bad for people and for profits. We need a rapid reversal of this trend and I believe that the principles behind *The Heart of Success* are absolutely vital to achieve it.'

Dr John Gallacher, psychologist and Senior Research Fellow,
University of Wales

'This is an excellent book, full of truth and wisdom. I would highly recommend it. It contains powerful, sobering, life-changing lessons that we should spend time to ponder on.'

Professor Leslie Lim, President, Singapore Association
of Mental Health

'So many of us crave for significance in our lives and in our work. This book opens up a way to finding it.'

John Evans, Senior Economist, Organisation for Economic
Co-operation and Development

'. . . an influential, recent book for executives who have it all in the workplace and not much outside of it.'

Wall Street Journal (*Europe*)

'I run a £200 million part of the BBC with more than 3,000 staff based at 50 different locations. I didn't have time to read Rob's book at work – it had to wait for my holiday! But I have tried very hard to apply his lessons since. Now I'm asking all my managers to focus on creating a culture of achievements, rather than long hours, for themselves and their teams too.'

Andy Griffee, Controller, BBC English Regions

'Parsons is unlike other business gurus . . . he identifies an emerging social class – the new poor.'

Des Dearlove, The Times

What they said about *The Sixty Minute Father* . . .

'Too often those of us heavily involved in the business world are in danger of losing out on our most important asset – our family. Reading *The Sixty Minute Father* reminded me of the opportunities I missed, and whilst I have been blessed with a loving family and two children, I know that this book will help me be a better grandfather.'

Sir Tom Farmer CBE, Chairman and Chief Executive, Kwik-Fit Holdings PLC

'Few people who have led successful lives have also achieved the most important success of all, namely of being a good father and taking part in the joys and extra dimensions that a close relationship with one's family can give. *The Sixty Minute Father* can help any executive get the balance right.'

Sir John Harvey-Jones MBE, Former Chairman of ICI and Management Consultant

'Surveys point to family neglect. Fathers prefer TV and gardening to time with their children. Rob Parsons, author of *The Sixty Minute Father*, said "I think fathers will regret it."'

Lucy Berrington, The Times

'Sixty minutes which could save the regret of lost family opportunities.'

Sally Wheale, The Guardian

'The theme of *The Sixty Minute Father* is simple: that today's dads have forgotten that the most important success of all is to be a good father.'

Anne Barrowclough, Sunday Mirror

THE MONEY SECRET

ROB PARSONS

Hodder & Stoughton
LONDON SYDNEY AUCKLAND

British Library Cataloguing in Publication Data
A record for this book is available from the British Library

ISBN 0 340 86277 7

Typeset in Garamond by Avon DataSet Ltd,
Bidford on Avon, Warwickshire

Printed and bound in Great Britain by
Bookmarque Ltd, Croydon, Surrey

The paper and board used in this paperback are natural recyclable
products made from wood grown in sustainable forests. The
manufacturing processes conform to the environmental regulations of
the country of origin.

Hodder & Stoughton
A Division of Hodder Headline Ltd
338 Euston Road
London NW1 3BH
www.madaboutbooks.com

To Jon Mason, who has been a fantastic encouragement to me and become a true friend.

Contents

Acknowledgements

Thank you to Sheron Rice – you made it a better book.

To Jonathan Booth for keeping me, and everybody else, at it.

To Lynda Reid and Katie Clarke for the brainstorming.

To Jon Mason for his input and ongoing encouragement.

To Judith Longman, my publisher at Hodder & Stoughton, who gave me her brilliant ideas (I hope I haven't spoiled them), helped me craft the book, and put me right without my ever knowing she'd done it.

And thanks also to: Andrew Buchanan-Smith, Samantha Callan, Bob Gorzynski, Kate Hancock, James Jamieson, Steve Williams, the team at Care for the Family, and all those who commented on the manuscript.

And finally thanks to Charles Nettleton, Julie Hatherall, Jean Whitnall, Patrick Knowles and the team at Hodder & Stoughton.

1
The Wishing Well

The tablets were in her handbag next to the brandy. She had intended to go straight back to her flat and take them there but for some reason she found herself turning right instead of left as she left the chemist and now she was on the edge of the park, just where it met the old cemetery. It was overcast and drizzling with rain as she walked through the gates and made her way towards the deserted children's play-area. She sat on the swing, immediately thinking that she had her best coat on and that whoever found her would say, 'She must have sat on something dirty before she died,' and then remembering that none of that mattered any more.

She opened the plastic container, took two tablets and a large swig of drink and let her eyes wander to the edge of the playground. And suddenly a hundred memories came flooding back. Just next to the slide was the wishing well. As a little girl she had thrown scores of pennies into its darkness and wished for things as varied as a sunny day, an exam success and a dog. She normally drank so little that the brandy was already making her feel light-headed and she stumbled as she got off the swing and walked towards the well. The weather-worn, graffiti-tormented plaque said, 'All Proceeds to our City's Children's Charities'. She sat on the edge of the well and fumbled in her pocket for the paracetamol. Her hand hit some loose change – it was from the chemist – and she grasped it and tossed it in.

A moment later she heard a voice – it must have belonged to somebody who had approached from the other side of the well. 'You didn't make a wish.'

The person who owned the voice was now at her side and Amy looked into old, sparkling eyes. With somebody younger she'd have told them where to go but she heard herself say, 'How do you know?'

'I just do,' said the older lady. 'If you *had* made a wish, what would it have been for?'

Amy was flummoxed. She fumbled in her pocket to make sure the tablets were still there, and turned the container over and over in her hand. She almost felt foolish, as if nobody could understand why a young woman would end her life over such a thing. She wanted to run – to find somewhere quiet and just do it. 'I owe a lot of money,' she said slowly, 'I can't pay them. There are too many.'

'And so what would you have wished for?'

'To be free of them all – to be free of debt.'

'There – you've wished it now! But you won't get it answered just by throwing money into a black hole – sometimes wishes need a little help for them to work. Have you got time for a cup of tea?'

Amy remembered wondering why old people always thought that a cup of tea could solve the ills of the world and then thinking that she could hardly say, no thank you, I have to rush. I'm going to kill myself. 'Why not?'

'There's a café round the corner, but first give me the rest of the tablets.'

For some reason that she couldn't quite remember, Amy passed over the container without protest and watched wide-eyed as the old lady emptied the whole lot into the well.

It wasn't until the older woman brought the tray of tea over that Amy looked properly at her. She wasn't as old as Amy had first thought – at least, she might not have been. In truth she could have been anything from mid-sixties to late seventies. And she was unusual, but at first Amy couldn't work out why. And then it dawned on her: the woman looked both wealthy and poor at the same time. Her clothes were old but they had obviously been expensive and her shoes were of fine leather – worn and shining. But it was more than this: she looked in control.

And everything she did seemed to be a contradiction. The way she ordered the tea was authoritative yet gracious. She asked if she could use a chair from a nearby table and Amy could have no more imagined the man refusing than if the Queen herself had asked for it. He had practically knocked his coffee over getting up to shift it for her.

'My name is Lydia,' she said, pouring the tea.

'I'm Amy.'

'Now, Amy, tell me about it – all of it.'

When Amy next looked at her watch she saw that two hours had passed. The man at the nearby table had long since left and the woman behind the counter was closing up. She saw that a fresh pot of tea had arrived but she couldn't remember either Lydia or herself ordering it. And she couldn't understand why she had told all that to a complete stranger: things she had never told her closest friends or her parents; things in some way she doubted she had ever told herself. It wasn't just how the debt had built up – leaving university with a student loan and an overdraft and then, over the next six years, adding another bank loan, six credit cards, two store cards, four catalogue debts, and over £600 in hire purchase goods. She'd told Lydia that she wasn't even sure what it all added up to; what she *was* sure of was how the debt had made her *feel*. For most of the time it made her feel afraid – afraid of what they all might do to her.

Sometimes she couldn't bring herself to open the bills and account statements. They made her feel ashamed, useless and helpless. And sometimes she felt stupid. As if somebody had said to her, 'How did you think you were going to repay it all?' It was like being in Maths at school when you were little and the teacher said, 'Seven sevens!' and you knew you should know the answer but you didn't. When she was small she had seen the look in a rabbit's eyes as the headlights from her father's car had caused it to freeze in the middle of a country road. She recalled the sickening thud and she remembered screaming, 'Why didn't it get out of the way?' And now she understood that it just couldn't. It was too scared to save itself.

'Debt makes us feel like that, my dear,' said Lydia. 'At first it's all quite wonderful. People seem to trust us enough to lend us money – it's even a little flattering that they want to do so. And in the beginning it doesn't feel like real money anyway, does it?'

'I feel ashamed of what I was about to do – I know many people are in so much more debt than me – it's just that the money troubles came at a difficult time anyway.'

'You don't need to explain. For many people debt is the trigger that leads to them seeking treatment for anxiety and depression.'[1]

'Apart from surviving at university I can't even tell you what I spent all the money on. If I could say, "It was the car" or "It was the holiday" it would still be stupid, but I'd know *what* it was – but I can't even do that. It was just things – clothes and CDs and cinema tickets and meals out. Just a lot of silly things.' Amy began to cry.

'It's not your fault,' said Lydia.

Amy felt angry but she wasn't sure at whom. 'Of course it's my fault! I needn't have applied for the cards or the overdraft, and I certainly didn't need to spend the money on a lot of rubbish. Plenty of people handle credit just fine.'

'Actually not many do, my dear; over six million families report some difficulties meeting their debt repayments.[2] Oh, I suppose you're not completely without blame, but offering all those credit cards to you was like awarding the fox the freedom of the farmyard and then complaining that he's had the chickens.'

For the first time in six months Amy heard herself laugh.

'I know that the banks and even some of the books on financial management say what you've just been saying yourself: banks, and credit card companies and the store card people are just providing a service; people have to be responsible. They don't force you to borrow money. But I don't agree, Amy, and if you'll let me, I'll show you why. Can you spend some time with me over the next few days?'

'I can, actually. I'm off work – have been for a while. But how can you help me?'

'I'll help you understand how you got into this mess in the first place, and when you get out of it this knowledge will keep you free of debt.'

'But how can I possibly get out of it?' Amy said.

'That will come later,' the older woman assured her. 'First, I'm going to show you how the whole system works. But before we start I want you to imagine you are back at the well and wishing again. Come on, indulge me – close your eyes.'

Amy did as she was told. 'What shall I ask for this time?'

'That you find the money secret!'

'I beg your pardon . . . ?'

'Amy, I am going to teach you much about money, but if you want to be free of debt for ever, knowledge will not be enough. I want you to find the secret.'

A moment later Amy opened her eyes.

'Good,' said Lydia, obviously satisfied. 'And now we must leave. I want to show you not just how to get out of debt, but what debt looks like, *feels* like, and why you have found it so very hard to escape it.'

'Where are we going?'

'Just trust me for now. Goodness, look at the time! We must fly!'

2
Know the Worst

Suddenly Amy was standing at the entrance to her own block of flats with Lydia next to her. Her head was still fuzzy from the combination of the alcohol and tablets, but even allowing for that she knew she would have remembered the journey from the park – if it had occurred. 'How . . . how did we get here?'

'Oh, don't worry about little things like that,' Lydia said, unconcerned. 'We'll need to do quite a bit of travelling like that over the next few days. You just concentrate on watching and listening.'

They entered the building and made their way

towards the lift. 'I live on the seventh floor,' Amy said, still trying to work out what had happened.

'Yes, I know,' came the reply.

'But . . .' Amy tried to form the question but was too tired and hit the call button instead. The aged lift groaned its way up the building. She saw that Lydia was looking at her intently.

'What are you thinking?'

'I was wondering how determined you are to be free of debt for ever – to truly be back in the black for a lifetime.'

'It mattered to me so much that I almost took my life.'

'I know,' Lydia touched Amy's arm. 'Well, we'll find out soon enough.'

The flat was small, comfortable and looked as though Amy had decided that whoever had the task of breaking the door down would at least find it tidy inside. She went to the kitchen to put the kettle on – it seemed that the financial guru she had brought home had an insatiable appetite for tea. When she came in with the tray she saw Lydia browsing through her bookshelves.

'I see you've been reading a lot about managing your money.'

'Yes, I've read four books on it,' Amy replied. 'Two of them are absolutely brilliant. They show you how to pick the best credit cards, how to move your balance to cards that don't charge you any interest at all for six months, how to time your purchases so that you get the best out of every card, and how you must always pay the full balance every month.'

'It sounds like good advice.'

'But it didn't help me, did it? I was useless at it.'

Lydia put her cup down. 'Amy, I only help people who want to be free of debt for ever. I come to people who are sick of debt, tired of the endless worry. If you and I are to work together it's very important that you understand something: I don't do financial management. I won't be teaching you how to juggle debt, move it around, caress it and love it. My aim is to make you *free* of it. I believe you could get out of debt *and* stay out of debt for ever.'

'I'll do anything you say.'

'Well, first of all I have a personal question for you,' Lydia said, warming to her task. 'Alongside your books on financial management I can see you've got a fair collection of diet books – though you don't look to me as if you need them! How much do you weigh?'

'That *is* personal – eight stone nine pounds.'

'And how often do you weigh yourself?'

'Once a week.'

'Why not once a year?'

'Because if I weigh myself once a week and I happen to have put on a few pounds I can do something about it quickly!' Amy knew something was coming but she wasn't sure what.

'And how much do you spend?'

'What do you mean? Daily, weekly, monthly or yearly?'

'You choose – tell me what you spend during any of those periods.'

'I don't know,' Amy admitted. 'All I know is that I spend too much.'

'Not good enough, Amy! If you really want to get free of debt you have to be as knowledgeable about your spending as you are about your weight. Do you think that for the rest of your life you will always know your weight within ten pounds?'

'I should hope so!'

'Well then, I want you to do the same for your spending. In future I want you to be able to know what you've spent to within £10 a week.'

'That's impossible!'

'No it's not!' Lydia said. 'I could find you any number of pensioners in the road outside who know exactly what they've spent this week. And it's not just possible for people on low incomes either – big businesses are the same. Do you think that an organisation like Microsoft wouldn't know what its weekly expenditure is?'

'Of course they would – but they have to produce accounts,' Amy protested.

'Exactly! The very poor and the very organised can do it week after week. If you are swimming in money it doesn't matter so much, but for most of us, not knowing how much we spend is a recipe for disaster. Come on, I'm going to put you on the financial weighing scales! Now, where do you keep your paperwork?'

Amy blushed. 'I don't really keep it anywhere in particular. There's some on the kitchen unit over there, some in those drawers and a fair number of bills just stuffed under the settee.'

Lydia was not easily put off. 'Well, never mind, collect as much as you can.'

It took all of half an hour but eventually there was a pile of papers on the kitchen table, some of them ripped, not a few coffee-stained, and all of them surprised at being disturbed.

Amy plucked up her courage. 'What do I do with this lot?'

'You're going to use them to help you fill in my "Reality Check" form. But before we start there's something we need. Do you mind if I have a little rummage in your kitchen?'

'Not at all,' replied Amy, bemused, as Lydia strode out of the room.

Amy could hear Lydia clattering about for quite a while, but finally she emerged from the kitchen holding an old biscuit tin that Amy had forgotten she had.

'This is perfect,' beamed Lydia.

'For what?'

'For our little project. I'm going to use it to collect

any forms, ideas and tips we come across, and by the time I present it to you at the end of our time together it will be quite full. And the first thing to go in it will be my "Reality Check" form.'† Lydia delved into her handbag and produced two pieces of paper.

'There we are! One for the tin and one for you to use now! We'll do the easy part first. Fill in all your income, starting with your salary. Put in your take-home pay rather than your salary before tax.'

'I can both start and end with my salary – I don't get anything else,' Amy said laughing, 'and even that will stop if I don't go back to work soon.'

'No other income at all?'

'Well, I know it sounds strange as I'm in so much debt, but since I was a kid doing a paper round I've had a savings account. I get a bit of interest every month from that but it's hardly worth putting in.'

'Put it down,' Lydia said firmly. 'We need every penny.'

---

† See 'The Biscuit Tin' at the end of the book for a copy of the 'Reality Check' form.

THAT'S THE WAY THE MONEY GOES

It didn't take long for Amy to fill in the income part of the form, and when that was done Lydia said, 'Now have a stab at the second part of the form – write "My Current Spending" at the top.'

Amy found this part much harder. It started off with costs to do with the home: 'Mortgage or rent', 'Second mortgage', 'Ground rent/service charge', 'Electricity', 'Gas', 'Water rates', 'Council tax', 'Buildings insurance', 'Home contents insurance'. Amy realised that she only had a vague idea of how much these were, and they had to sort through the stack of papers to find bills for each one.

The next heading was 'Housekeeping' – this included food for eating at home, cleaning supplies and toiletries. Then there was 'TV licence', 'Telephone', 'Mobile phone', 'Meals out/takeaways', 'Entertainment', 'Prescription costs', 'Emergencies' and quite a few other items as well. She found a few of them difficult to work out, but some were on her credit card statements, there were odd receipts for others and with the rest she took an educated guess.

Lydia nodded her approval and then said, 'Not bad; now let's have a look at a bank statement.'

'Easier said than done, actually,' Amy was forced to admit. 'I don't usually keep them.'

Lydia took a deep breath. 'I see. Well, from now on I suggest that you keep them very carefully. In a file, perhaps. In fact, if your bank will send you weekly statements instead of monthly ones without charging you any extra, I think you should get them to do so. One of the big keys to staying in financial control is up-to-date information.'

As Lydia had been speaking she had been rifling through the stack of papers again and now waved one aloft. 'I thought I'd noticed it in there,' she said triumphantly. 'One bank statement – four months old, but it'll do. Put in the expenditure from all the standing orders and direct debits that you haven't already entered.' Lydia scoured the statement and pointed to several entries. 'What are these?'

'Those are cash – where I use the hole in the wall.'

'Yes, I thought so. On a financial diet, cash is the equivalent of snacking at the fridge. There's an entry almost every day – what do you spend all this cash on?'

'Oh, I don't know – it's just everyday things. For example, I normally have a coffee on the way to work.'

'What does that cost?'

'It's about £1.20. And then I buy sandwiches and a can of drink for my lunch – that's about £3.50.'

'And you do that most working days?'

'Yes.'

Lydia produced a calculator from her bag. In went the daily coffee, sandwich and drink, multiplied by 220 for the working days in a year. 'So you're spending just over £1,000 a year on those,' she said when the sum had been done.

Amy sucked in her breath. 'That can't be right!'

'I assure you it is, and what's more, because you have to pay this amount out *after* you have paid tax and national insurance on it, you actually have to earn over £1,300 a year just to pay for your coffees and sandwiches!'

They carried on working through the form, and at last Lydia seemed satisfied that Amy had made a reasonable effort at estimating her spending. 'What I want you to do now is add up the "Spending" section.

And when you've done that, I want you to compare that figure with the one in your "Income" part and tell me the difference.'

Amy knew without doing the maths which way the scales would fall, but it was still a shock when she saw by how much. 'I can't believe it!' she said, leaning back in the chair. 'I'm paying out over £100 more than I've got coming in *every* month.'

Lydia didn't seem surprised. 'That's about what I thought it would be,' she said. 'Most people I meet spend at least 10 per cent more than they earn.'

CUTTING BACK

Delving into her bag again Lydia produced another copy of the 'Reality Check' form and put it on the table in front of Amy. 'Here's the next step: fill the "Income" in again, the same as before, but this time head the "Spending" part "My Goal" and look at every category to see if it can be reduced. The aim is that the total of this section will be *less* than you earn. In other words, you're going on a financial diet.'

'But how can I do that?' Amy complained. 'I don't have an extravagant lifestyle. What can I cut out?'

'Obviously there are some figures you won't be able to change at all – the council tax, electricity, water rates – things like that,' Lydia explained, 'but a good place to start would be to have another look at that bank statement. We'll start with the easy ones – the direct debits and standing orders. Explain to me what each of these is.'

'Well, that's the mortgage,' said Amy pointing out a figure of almost £600, 'and that's council tax, that one is the water rates, and . . .'

'What's this one of £52 a month?' Lydia interrupted.

'That's my gym.'

'I must admit I've never belonged to one – what do you do there?'

'I walk, mostly.'

Lydia looked up from the bank statement. 'Where do you walk?'

'I don't walk anywhere – it's just on a conveyor belt.'

'Why don't you walk outside? It's free!'

'Well . . .' Amy felt a little defensive. 'Sometimes it's cold or raining.'

For the first time that day Lydia looked un-sympathetic. 'What else do you do there?'

'I cycle.'

'Where do you cycle?'

'I don't cycle anywhere – it's just on a stationary machine.' Amy thought she knew what was coming, but Lydia moved on without comment.

'How often do you go there?'

Amy's face began to flush a little. 'When I first joined I used to go two or three times a week but now I sometimes only go once a month.'[1]

Lydia pursed her lips, 'Amy, if I owned that health club I would sit in an office overlooking the entrance and when you came up the drive I would yell out, "Quick, put the red carpet out – here comes the customer who pays us over £600 a year, to come here once a month to walk nowhere and cycle nowhere!" Are there any more members like you?'

'Quite a lot,' Amy said, thinking it over. 'I think most of us intend to start getting fit, but never actually get around to it. I suppose that keeping the membership going is a way of easing the guilt.'

'Cancel it immediately,' Lydia said firmly. 'You'll save over £600 a year. I'm sure for that kind of money you can live with the guilt of not walking on a conveyor belt once a month.' The matter dealt with, she returned to Amy's bank statement. 'Now, what's this sum of £60 a month?'

'It's insurance on my hi-fi, the TV and DVD player, my fridge and my freezer. I've bought them all since I moved into the flat. It covers me in case they break down.'

'Cancel it!'

Lydia laughed when she saw Amy's face. 'Yes – I mean it. Cancel it right away. And do the same with this one, too, for home plumbing and central heating cover.'

'I really don't get it,' said Amy, looking genuinely confused. 'Surely having protection for breakdowns and things going wrong with your heating is sensible?'

Lydia ignored her but continued to scan the bank statement. 'What's this standing order for £22?'

'It's pet insurance in case my dog gets ill.'

'Amy, if your dog ever works out the real cost of his cover he'll get ill just thinking about it. Cancel it!'

Amy looked worried. 'I know what you're thinking,' Lydia said, catching her expression. 'What if the water pipes burst on to the hi-fi, and in the ensuing flood the dog catches pneumonia?'

Amy smiled. 'Something like that.'

'Amy, I want you to be in a position to have savings to cover these emergencies when they occur – but just now you simply can't afford to shell out all this money – you just don't have it.'

The next standing order on the statement was for £25 to a savings account. 'That's the one I mentioned to you that I've had since I was a kid,' Amy explained. 'I've been quite proud of myself for keeping it going all this time and it's got me out of one or two holes over the years.'

'Having some kind of savings or investments is definitely a good idea,' Lydia replied, 'but right now it's got to go on your "Cancel Immediately" list.' Amy looked aghast but Lydia continued, 'Let me explain. How much interest does it give you?'

Searching through the papers, Amy found a statement and handed it over. 'Yes, it's what I thought,' Lydia said. 'This savings account is paying you interest of just 2 per cent, and yet your current account – where you're paying those savings from –

is in overdraft with an interest rate of 12 per cent. It means that you're borrowing money at 12 per cent interest so that you can pay it into a savings account which gives you 2 per cent interest. Instead of saving money, you're losing it at a rate of 10 per cent a year!'

Amy was quiet and Lydia guessed her thoughts. 'Amy, don't be too hard on yourself. There are plenty of people investing in the stock market right now, hoping for gains of between 7 per cent and 10 per cent, who at the same time have credit card debt at 19 per cent.'

Lydia's second form was still lying untouched on the table but now Amy felt ready to take a stab at it. Twenty-five minutes later, and surrounded by balls of crunched-up paper, she was finished. With a final tap on the calculator she looked up. 'When I stop all the direct debits and standing orders on the "Cancel Immediately" list, I'll have saved £240 a month. You just don't realise where it all goes.'

'Exactly. Do you know the comment most people make at diet clubs when they get on the scales and have put on a little weight?'

Amy laughed – everybody knew it. 'Yes, they say, "I don't understand it – I haven't cheated at all!"'

'And what does the dietician do in those circumstances?'

'She'd make you write down everything you eat.'

'Exactly,' Lydia said again. 'And that's why, for the next month, I want you to write down everything that you spend using cash. I want you to get used to how much you spend, and the very act of writing it down will make you think twice about spending it in the first place. When you're on a strict financial diet and keeping a close track of it, a new CD or a pair of shoes you don't really need shows up like a cream doughnut in a slimming class!'

'That's going to be a real pain,' Amy grumbled. 'And anyway, what about spending on credit cards?'

'You won't have to worry about those for reasons that will soon become plain,' Lydia said cheerfully.

Amy could guess the reasons pretty easily and thought of the film and music club she joined three years ago. It had been a pretty good deal getting the six CDs for practically nothing, and it was definitely cheaper to buy from the club, but as she glanced at her CD rack she knew she hadn't listened to half of them more than once. The combination of the monthly magazine, a telephone and her credit card had been a pretty lethal one.

'OK, OK, I admit it! I just like buying things. I think it's a kind of reaction against my father. He always takes ages to think things through before buying anything more expensive than a tube of toothpaste! He wouldn't know the meaning of the phrase "impulse buying". But he's right, I know. I'm just a dead loss. I mean, he's in his fifties now and has never been in debt in his life.'

Lydia shook her head. 'No, you're nowhere near a dead loss, Amy, and anyway there are times when doing things on impulse isn't such a bad thing. Besides, I believe it was probably a little easier for your father's generation to stay out of debt.'

'Why do you say that?'

'Because just about the time that you were born, the weapons changed.'

'What weapons?'

'What weapon do you think revolutionised warfare in our world?'

'The gun, I suppose.'

'Yes, and after that, the Gatling gun. For thousands of years weaponry was essentially swords, bows, arrows and the odd catapult. There were two big disadvantages with all those: first, you had to get pretty close to the enemy – and that's never a good idea – and second, you could normally only kill the opposition one at a time. But all of a sudden a weapon emerged that could fire 1,200 rounds a minute! One person could now keep a small army at bay. The problem is that sometimes armies take a while to adjust to the fact that their enemy has made a little progress, and they continue to use the old tactics. When that happens, you have soldiers going over the top in manoeuvres that were effective against rifles, but disastrous against the Gatling.'

Amy began to wonder where all this was leading. 'What's that got to do with my father and debt?'

'Well, as I said a moment ago, about twenty-five years ago the shopping weapons changed. The new ones have totally revolutionised how easy it is for people to spend money and therefore get into debt. If we shoppers are to avoid the debt pitfalls, we need to recognise the new weapons and change our tactics a little. I'm going to show you how it works tomorrow, but right now I think we both need a good night's sleep – we've worked pretty hard today.' Lydia pulled on her coat and made her way to the door. 'Shall I pick you up here in the morning for a visit to the supermarket?'

'How could I refuse an offer like that?'

3

Choose Your Weapons

Amy's head definitely wasn't fuzzy this time, but it happened again the next morning. One minute she'd been in the flat with Lydia, and now they were standing on a balcony in a large supermarket. They were near the manager's office, looking down on the crowded store. Lydia saw her concern. 'Don't worry about a thing, Amy – nobody can see us.'

'What do you mean, nobody can see . . . ? And, anyway, how did we . . . ?'

'I said not to worry about that. Now isn't this fascinating – the supermarket is a good example of the way that the shopping weapons have changed. People used to buy their groceries from small suppliers, and usually went in with a list made up after working out how much money they could spend on food that week. The goods were displayed on shelves, but often the grocer had to get them from the back of the shop because there just wasn't room to show them all.'

'There's plenty of room here!' Amy said, looking at the size of the store.

'Yes – and do you see what shopping lists have been replaced by?'

Amy could see one or two people with bits of paper in their hands, but not many. 'No, sorry.'

'Trolleys!' said Lydia. 'We now shop by looking, liking and lifting!'

'You make it sound like a crime!' Amy said.

'I'm sure you know what I mean. Many of us start off with good intentions and a determination to only buy what we need, but then we start "grazing" – looking around for what we fancy and sweeping it into the trolley. And when we've finished walking up and down every aisle in the shop, we stop grazing and find a till. The problem is that we've only got a very rough idea of how much everything we've collected is going to cost us. What game do you often see people play at the check-out?'

'Guess the total cost of the trolley!'

'Yes. And anything within £10 is a pretty good guess. Now answer this. Even if supermarkets had existed at the time, why couldn't previous generations have shopped like that?'

'I suppose it was because they had to be sure that they had enough money on them to pay for what they bought.'

'Exactly. And that's where another new retailing weapon comes into its own – the credit card. The credit card allows you to graze, to put in the trolley anything you fancy and not worry whether you have enough money to pay for it today. We have long since stopped using credit cards just for special purchases. In fact almost 25 per cent now use credit and loans to pay for basic household expenses.'[1]

'You sound as if you'd like to take us back to the Dark Ages.'

'Amy, if you told your grandparents (who often had

their groceries delivered to their front door by a man in a small van) that one day people would have to get their shopping by walking around a huge building, pushing a gigantic trolley with a mind of its own, collecting the goods from the shelves themselves, queuing for ten minutes to pay for it, packing it all into bags, and then loading it again into the rebellious trolley so they can push the thing to their car, where the whole process starts again, they'd have thought *this* was the Dark Ages! But enough of that. It's time to look at the next weapon and it's right under our noses: the megastore.'

'What do you mean by that?'

'Well, it's all under one roof. Just look down – you might come in here for a packet of tea and some biscuits, but soon you're looking at fridges, cookers, televisions, clothes, holidays, dry cleaning, life insurance, loans and a pharmacy!'

'But surely that's all good? It's giving customers a tremendous service.'

'It is in some ways, but when new weapons are around to get you to part with your money you need to have some weapons of your own to launch a defence. And the most important one is in between your ears! Look – can you see that couple over there?' Lydia pointed to a man and woman in their late twenties who were engrossed in conversation in the 'Homeware' section.

'They only came in to do the weekly shop but he got bored and wandered into the electrical section. And now he's trying to persuade his wife to buy a wide-screen television. They don't have the money saved to make the purchase, and their credit cards are up to the limit, but help is at hand and the salesperson is about to bring out a retailing weapon that has made many people buy something they just can't afford – "interest-free credit"!' Lydia turned to the younger woman. 'When I first started out, an old man gave me some good advice. I'd like you to remember it: "Don't let anybody do anything for nothing – it's too expensive!"'

Amy laughed. 'How can something that's free be expensive?'

'Just watch. Let's listen as the salesman reels them in.'

SALESMAN: That's not a problem – you don't have to put any deposit down and there's no interest at all for six months!

WOMAN: No, I don't think so, Jack. We just can't afford it at the moment.

MAN: But why not? Think of what we're saving by not paying any interest.

'Did you hear that?' Lydia broke in. 'The bit about "saving"? He's about to spend over £800 on something that in a month's time he won't be able to sell for £400 and already he's talking about "saving"!'

The two women continued to watch and listen as the wife put up a brave fight for ten minutes or so but finally shrugged her shoulders and gave in. The salesman smiled and took some forms from under the sales counter.

'What are those?' Amy asked.

'It's a loan agreement.'

'But I thought it was "interest-free"?' Amy said, puzzled, and then, as she saw Lydia's eyebrows lift, 'Come on, tell me.'

Lydia sighed deeply. 'They are about to sign a loan

agreement at an interest rate of 29 per cent over four years.[2] If they repay in full within the six-month period it's true there will be no interest and nothing else to pay.'

'But where will they get the money in six months?'

'Where indeed? That's exactly how this particular weapon works. If they are *one* day over the six months, interest at that very high rate will be added going right back to today – in other words, the interest-free period will be scrapped and they will be left with a run-of-the mill interest-bearing loan.'

Amy was thinking rapidly. 'But I know of some furniture companies that not only give interest-free loans, they offer no payments at all for a year.'

'It's just a variation on the trick,' Lydia responded. 'You're not saving anything because their furniture is more expensive to begin with than comparable furniture in other shops.'

'But they offer it in their sales,' Amy protested.

'Amy, haven't you noticed that some shops have rather a lot of sales? But let's get back to this couple. Do you remember that they came in to do their weekly shop and they've already bought a wide-screen television? And the salesman isn't through with them yet. He's about to separate them from even more of their hard-earned money, and to do so he's going to use one of the most effective of the modern retailing weapons. Here it comes now – listen hard.'

SALESMAN: I can also offer you a discount on our special extended three-year guarantee. This will cover the television if it breaks down – labour and parts – and if we can't mend it we'll give you a new one. It even covers you if you accidentally smash the screen. It's just £55 a year and you don't have to pay now. I can add it to the interest-free loan for you.

Amy was puzzled. 'I know you've told me to stop the insurance cover I've had on some of my things – and I can see that I can't afford it right now – but surely an extended guarantee on an £800 television has got to be a good thing to buy?'

'Amy, there's only one thing that makes less sense than making purchases on credit and that's signing up for the extended guarantee as well! An Office of Fair Trading investigation found that some firms were charging up to 50 per cent of the purchase price for extended guarantees on goods that in some cases rarely broke down.[3] Put yourself in the retailer's place. They know that consumers are very price-sensitive and that they'll shop around for the best price – if one retailer's television is more expensive than their competitor's, they won't sell it – so they've got to get some extra revenue from somewhere. Enter the extended guarantee.' Lydia was on a roll now and Amy was desperately trying to take in what she was saying.

'The manufacturer probably already gives you twelve months' warranty on most consumer goods, and the retailer knows that most goods that break down (especially electronics and things like cookers or washing machines) do so either in the first twelve months (when they are covered by the warranty anyway) or years later. The chances of a customer needing to use an extended warranty in the first three years are therefore extremely small.'

'But it's comforting to have the protection – and there have been times when I have used it.'

'So, here's what you should do,' said Lydia. 'When

you buy something on which you would like a guarantee, *don't* take the extended one offered by the retailer. Instead, put the amount you would have paid on the warranty into a separate account. As you do that for various items – cookers, freezers, hi-fi systems – you'll build up quite a fund and you'll find that if you do need a repair on one of them, you'll quite likely have enough in the fund not only to repair it, but to replace it. And if the money isn't used – it's yours to do as you like with.'

They continued to watch as the salesman added the sum for the extended warranty to the cost of the television, which brought it to almost £1,000. Then he added the cost of the interest if the couple were not able to repay it all after six months. The total cost of the loan was over £1,500. Both the man and the woman signed the agreement.

'And that, my dear,' said Lydia, 'is why it's a little harder for you to stay out of debt than it was for your father.'

'But what can we do about it?'

FIGHTING BACK

'Well, it's hard. Most of us have been woefully prepared to deal with the revolution that has occurred in shopping and credit – just look at all those people collecting their loyalty points.'

'What's wrong with them?' Amy said in disbelief. 'I've been collecting them for years.'

'Well, Amy, some of them work well, but most aren't worth much. Stores know that customers are price-sensitive – everybody can read the price of a can of beans – so the idea of loyalty points is to take the customer's eye off the price and make them want to keep shopping with you to build up other rewards.

'I suppose at their best you get a little extra for shopping with a store that you would have used anyway, but at their worst you shop at a more expensive outlet just to build up the points. It may take a year to build up enough points to earn a hairdryer! The better strategy is to make sure that when you shop, you purchase only what you need and from the very cheapest supplier. That way you don't save points, you save money – probably enough to get your hairdryer in a fortnight!'

Amy laughed so loud she thought the manager would come out of his office. 'I saved a year for a set of saucepans!' she admitted.

'Well, it's just another of the modern retail weapons I've been telling you about. Here's another – the weapon of confusion. Someone coined the term "confusopoly" to explain what goes on in modern marketing. The idea is that firms confuse the customer as to what any particular deal is worth and especially how it compares to other offers in the market.[4] Financial services companies love confusopolies.

'There's so much confusing detail, I guarantee that a roomful of a hundred lawyers and accountants wouldn't be able to agree on the best mortgage available,' Lydia continued. 'So if you're finding it confusing deciding between "deals", don't for a moment believe that the problem is you. You are looking at a confusopoly!

'And supermarkets love to play confusopoly too. If you want to find the very cheapest goods in most supermarkets then you'd better be Einstein – or at least have time on your hands to look at all the special offers – buy-one-get-one-free, money-off coupons and "today's special discounts". And it's not just the prices; the goods themselves are confusing! What do you think one of the main diet breakfast cereals is?'

Amy answered in a heartbeat, 'Special K!'

'Right. Now name me a breakfast cereal that you would never eat if you were trying to lose weight.'

'Frosties.'

'Well, you'd think so, yes,' Lydia agreed. 'But if we picked up a box of Special K and a packet of Frosties and read the nutritional information on the sides of the packaging, we'd find that the two cereals have about the same number of calories and that Frosties has less fat content than Special K.'

'But why did Kelloggs choose Special K as the slimming cereal?' Amy asked.

'If you eat a breakfast cereal and keep an eye on your weight, Special K is probably as good as most, and perhaps marginally better than some others,' Lydia conceded. 'But it's nothing like the big deal that it's portrayed as. Next time you see a special "slimming" food, compare the nutritional information on the side of the packet or can with that of the cheaper "normal" variety; if there's not much difference between them, then juggle the normal one for a minute or two to burn off the few extra calories and buy that!'

'Lydia – why does nobody tell us about all of this?'

'Well, of course, you're right. We'd probably do our young people more good teaching them some of this instead of "Sheep farming in Australia". And much of it is simply having your eyes opened to what's going on. But a major step forward is when we begin to fight back with a few weapons of our own. Here are three, and any one of them would save most of the people in this supermarket enormous amounts of money over a year.

'Number one: recognise the power of a list. Make a list of what you want to buy when you go out shopping and stick to it.

'Number two: recognise the power of a sum. Set a financial limit for the shopping trip and calculate as you go how much money you have left.'

'You mean walk around the supermarket with a calculator?' Amy interrupted.

'Why not? Amy, for goodness' sake, I'm only talking about making sure you have enough money to pay for what you've bought. When did that become either boring or radical?

'Number three: recognise the power of impulse buying. This is the really big one,' Lydia said, 'and I wouldn't mind betting it's the main reason why you've got into so much debt.'

Lydia looked as if she was about to move on so Amy spoke: 'I know that you're right – especially about impulse buying – but do you mind if I ask you a question?'

'Anything,' said Lydia.

'Do you ever get called a kill-joy?'

Lydia laughed. 'All the time! And you know what I say? Kill-joy? I'll tell you how to kill joy! Get somebody into a shop to buy their weekly groceries and send them out with a wide-screen television they don't need, can't afford and which will break down the day after the ridiculously expensive extended warranty you sold them ends. And when you've done all of that, write to them the day after their six-month interest-free period finishes and tell them that the direct debit they signed will now increase because you are going to start adding interest at some outrageous rate – going back to the very start of the agreement – and that it will take them four years to pay it all off. No, Amy, I'm not in the same league as the real kill-joys!

'But now it's time for one of the really big lessons,' Lydia went on. 'Do you remember what you said to me when we first spoke in the café about what you had spent all that money on?'

'Well . . . I said I couldn't remember most of it. It was just a lot of silly *things.*'

'That's exactly right,' said Lydia and with that she took hold of Amy's arm. 'Let's go a little way up the road – there's something I want to show you . . .'

4

Retail Therapy

The journey above the dual carriageway took just seconds, and this time Amy took it in her stride. She found herself standing with Lydia on the first floor of a vast shopping centre. A vaulted glass ceiling towered above them.

'This is taking what we just saw in the supermarket to its ultimate,' Lydia said. 'Here you have many shops all under one roof. If you enter this mall to find a shop that sells wool and knitting needles you have to pass others that sell every variety of goods. It's laid out in precise terms – the position of the food-halls,

the department stores, and the layout of the floors –
all to keep us under that amazing roof and get us to
visit as many shops as possible. What can you smell?'

'Great coffee!' said Amy.

'That's no accident. When they build these places
they calculate carefully the position of the coffee
shops – they know the aroma makes us feel good,
and when we feel good, we buy! By the way, can you
see the "down" escalator?'

Amy said she couldn't. 'No,' Lydia agreed, looking
round as well, 'and you won't until you've had a long
walk and passed another twenty shops! It's why, at
airports, you often have to walk through the duty-free
shop to get to your gate, and why, in many
supermarkets, the bread and milk are at the back of
the store and often separated from each other. Almost
everybody buys bread and milk and they want to
make sure you have to walk past as many other
goods as possible before you get to them. Those who
design shops these days don't concentrate on getting
you to spend money on what you came in for – but
on things that didn't even enter your head when you
left your house.'

Amy wasn't convinced. Her eyes darted around the mall. 'But shopping is such fun!'

'It wasn't much fun when I met you,' Lydia shot back. 'Do you remember what you told me a moment ago?'

'Yes – that I couldn't even remember what I'd spent all the money on.'

'Amy, shopping malls *are* fun!' said Lydia, relenting a little. 'But remember, the plan is to get you to impulse buy. Don't! I often think of those adverts for cosmetics and hair products that end with the phrase, "Because you're worth it!" I want you to believe that, but to add a word to it – "anyway". You don't have to prove you are somebody by what you own or wear. When God made you He didn't make a mistake. You are worth it whether you buy that dress or don't, splash out on that gadget or not, drive the latest car or one that's ten years old. You, Amy, are worth it – anyway!'

Amy looked as if she might cry but Lydia wasn't stopping for emotional breaks. 'Over the next few days you will meet some very poor people. It's my view that they simply don't have enough income, but for most of us that's not the problem. We *do* have enough money; we just spend too much – on a lot of "silly things". Amy, there's an aspect of debt that most of us don't even want to consider but it's the reason why systems to sort your finances out are not usually enough, and why, despite very good intentions, many people never manage to break free of debt.'

'It sounds ominous.'

'It is. Tell me, have you ever smoked?'

Amy nodded. 'Yes, in my late teens and early twenties.'

'But you've given up now?'

'Yes – absolutely.'

'Was it easy?'

'It was one of the hardest things I've ever done; it took me five attempts!'

'Amy, think why it was so hard to give up. I expect you'd read the medical advice and watched reports on television about people who died because of smoking. You've probably got relatives who have been affected by it. So why didn't you just stop?'

'Well, first it was especially hard because when I was trying to give up, all my friends were still smoking. But it was more than that; it wasn't until I tried to stop that I realised I was totally addicted.'

Lydia nodded. 'Remember those two reasons, Amy: peer pressure and addiction. They are the very same ones that make it so difficult for millions of people to escape from debt. In fact, it's that second one I want us to look at now.'

THE SHOPPING FIX

'Don't tell me that *shopping* is addictive,' Amy said, laughing.

But Lydia wasn't joining in the merriment – always a danger sign. 'Can you remember the wording on the little plaque you have hanging in your kitchen?'

Amy felt herself blush. 'When the going gets tough, the tough go shopping!'

'Yes,' said Lydia, 'and the sad thing is that for many people that saying has become a reality. In fact psychiatrists are beginning to talk about a new disorder[1] – and there's already a dictionary definition for it. It's made up of two words: "retail" – the selling of goods to the public – and "therapy" – the treatment of a physical or mental problem.'[2]

'Retail therapy!' laughed Amy. 'Shop till you drop.'

'Actually, "shop *when* you drop – emotionally" sums it up better! The dictionary defines it as "the act of shopping in order to relax or make yourself feel better".'[3]

'I think people make too much of all that – after all, it's just shopping.'

Lydia looked pensive for a while and then turned to the younger woman. 'Take my hand for a moment.'

'What?'

'Just trust me – take my hand.'

Amy did as Lydia asked and reached out towards her. She was not able to remember exactly what happened after that, except that suddenly they were looking down on a huge city from a very great height. Hundreds of shops were sprawled out beneath them. The retail section of the town was built around a square dominated by a vast neon display showing the date, time and temperature. The time was right, the temperature seemed a little out, but the date was definitely wrong – four whole months wrong! She was about to ask Lydia what was happening when the older woman said, 'Look in that shop down there.'

Amy felt Lydia's grip on her hand tighten and they zoomed in on a single figure in a department store.

The woman they were watching was carrying several bags, each with the name of a different shop on it, and they watched as she flicked aimlessly through a rack of tops.

Amy's face whitened. She had no doubt who they were observing, but the figure seemed so lonely. It was as if, in an instant, she was able to feel again the emotions of that day. 'That's me, isn't it?' she said, brushing her hand across her eyes.

'Yes, but it's not *just* you – millions of us shop like that. Can you remember why you bought all those things that day?'

'Of course I can't. It wasn't any special occasion or anything like that. And before you go on about "retail therapy" let me tell you that it was one of the few days in the past six months when I felt pretty good for a couple of hours.'

'Amy, this isn't just about going shopping because you feel depressed. It's about the fact that for some people the very act of buying things has become a kind of drug to help them get through life; and, of course, you take more of it when you're down, but in truth you need a fix most weeks.'

Amy shook her head. 'I just can't take all this in. You make it sound as if I've got some kind of illness.'

'Some of us have. Research has shown that unhappy people are most likely to try to change their lives by changing their diet, their appearance or their homes – and all that involves buying things.'[4]

'But it doesn't work! Sometimes I would drag all that stuff home and completely lose interest in it – it would just stay in the bags for days.'

'That's exactly what the research showed,' Lydia agreed. 'In fact, one woman who was interviewed said, "I go shopping when I feel low to cheer myself up. It does make me feel better, but only for that night really. Often having spent the money makes me feel worse later on."'[5]

'So why do we do it?'

'For many reasons: perhaps it makes us feel special when at that time in our lives nobody else is paying us much attention, or perhaps it's just that it helps us to escape reality for a while.'

'It never even crossed my mind that that might have

been why I was spending so much – all those CDs, shoes and I don't know what other junk I didn't need.' Again, Amy looked as if she might cry. 'But what can I do about it?'

'Well, first don't get too steamed up if there's no need to; treating ourselves once in a while is no bad thing. But if we are regularly buying things we never use or don't really need, it's worth asking why. Sometimes, just noticing what's going on can help us change. One woman realised that an old grief had triggered her spending sprees, and when that dawned on her she cut up her credit cards there and then.'[6]

For a while neither of them said anything, they just watched as the woman in the store pulled a red top from the rack, took it to the counter and paid for it with her store card.

Amy spoke first. 'I didn't expect all this when we started. I just thought you would teach me to handle my money better.'

'Amy, your main problem wasn't that you couldn't handle money,' Lydia said gently. 'If that was the only reason people got into debt there wouldn't be a chartered accountant in the land in financial trouble –

and trust me there are some. Do you remember the promise I made you at our very first meeting?'

'You said you'd help me understand how I got into this mess in the first place – so I could be free of it for ever.'

'I did indeed – and that means knowing about a lot more than budget forms and systems. Now, are you ready for a little light relief?'

'Definitely.'

'Well, take my hand again. If retail therapy is real and shopping is sometimes a drug, I want to show you some of the pushers!'

CREDIT CARD CURES FOR THE 'BLUES MEANIES'

And with that Lydia was off – and Amy behind her. It seemed only seconds later that they had stopped and were standing in the foyer of a five-star hotel. Lydia pointed to some easy chairs in the corner of a lounge area. 'Go and put your feet up – I'll be back in a moment.'

When Lydia returned she had a clutch of papers in her hands. One was a leaflet advertising the hotel's spa facilities. She handed it to Amy. 'I told you it was time for a little light relief. Read out the bit at the bottom.'

Amy started to read, and as she went on they both began giggling like schoolgirls:

There is nothing like a change of scenery, stylish surroundings and a day of shopping to satisfy your every craving. Enjoy a little retail therapy with an appointment with the personal shopping assistant at a top department store. The aim of your visit is to spoil yourself with choice. Included in what can only be described as an alternative therapy experience is one night's accommodation and breakfast and a personal chauffeur to take you shopping. On your return to the hotel enjoy a Champagne Afternoon Tea to celebrate your purchases.[7]

By the time she had finished reading they were laughing so much that Amy thought they'd be asked to leave. 'Celebrate your purchases!' shrieked Lydia as she passed over another piece of paper. 'And this is from one of the on-line shopping channels. Read out that bit,' she said, pointing to a picture of a woman who looked like Michelle Pfeiffer.

Amy did as she was told. The company's shopping editor was giving some 'credit card cures' for an attack of the 'blues meanies'.[8]

Spending over £70 on a bra may seem like a rather reckless indulgence which is why I heartily recommend you slap down that credit card right now and go for it.[9]

They both giggled out loud again but then Amy said, 'I know we're laughing, Lydia, but it would be a dull world if you couldn't splash out occasionally.'

'I agree.'

'Do you really?'

'Of course I do. But when you do decide to indulge yourself a little I want you to know exactly what's going on and do it because you want to, not just because you're getting sucked into making some purchase you don't really want or need and – even worse – that will bring you little pleasure.'

'But, Lydia, this is all just a bit of fun; surely even the advertisers understand that?'

'Amy, don't you believe it. Those who sell goods know how we feel – our fears, our insecurities, our desire to be special – and of course they play on those emotions. One psychologist said that the very purpose of some advertising is to make us feel discontent with our bodies and personalities. And when we're a little depressed we're especially vulnerable. In fact, one study showed that people who felt depressed were twice as likely to have bought something and regretted it later.'[10]

Amy thought back to the solitary woman buying the top in the department store. 'The funny thing is, Lydia, you buy all this stuff to feel better, to look better – often to impress others – to be part of the crowd, but when the debt comes it's the loneliest feeling in the world; then it's just you.'

Lydia took Amy's hand. 'Listen to me carefully. If I help you get out of debt and in the process rob you of fun, spontaneity and the ability to spoil yourself once in a while, I'll have failed. But when you go shopping I want it to be on *your* terms, not dancing to the tune of some advertiser, credit card company or shopping editor who offers you a £70 bra or a "set of golf clubs to make your friends green with envy" as a cure for your "blues meanies".'

Amy smiled. 'Lydia, you don't have to worry about my thinking you're trying to rob me of fun – I've laughed more with you in the last couple of days than in the past year.'

'Just remember some of the lessons. One woman put it well: "Retail Therapy is the equivalent of a throat lozenge when what we need is ointment for the soul."[11] You and I are worth more than the accumulation of what we own. Unless we understand that we will never be able to deal with the problem of debt.'

' "Ointment for the soul",' repeated Amy. 'I like that.'

They sat for a while in silence and then Amy spoke. 'You look tired – let's go home and get a cup of tea.'

'No, I'm fine,' said Lydia, 'and actually, on the way back to your flat, I want us to take a little diversion via the waterfront. There's somebody I've promised to visit and I'd very much like you to come with me . . .'

5
First Things First

They stood together at what was once a dockside. On the right-hand side of the road, overlooking the water, apartment blocks soared into the sky from every angle. They had been advertised as 'unique' and yet to Amy's eye they all seemed strangely similar, as if some demented architect had been given a lorryload of wood, chrome and reproduction ships' anchors and told to use the lot. Nevertheless, they were impressive – and very expensive.

But not all the dwellings in the area were so chic. On the left-hand side of the road were the remnants of the housing estate that used to dominate the docks. Here there was no chrome or wood, and not an anchor in sight. Paint peeled off the walls, old cars – many of them, it seemed, never to move again – filled the spaces outside the houses or, in some cases, the small patch of concrete in what the original planners had rather hopefully called 'the front garden'.

Amy gazed up at the new apartment blocks on the right-hand side of the road. Expensive cars lined the parking bays outside, and nearby the new trendy restaurants were already filling up. 'I'll bet there's not much debt on that side of the road!' she commented.

'Unfortunately that's not true,' Lydia replied. 'In fact, at the end of our time together we'll have to cross the road; it is there we will find the money secret.'

'I was hoping we'd be able to find it today,' Amy said, but Lydia just smiled, turned sharp left and began walking into the heart of the old docklands. The younger woman hurried to catch her up.

Amy heard the crying before she even entered the house. Not so much crying as wailing – a haunting cry of despair that wafted over the terraced houses. And suddenly she was looking at her – a woman who lay curled up like a baby on the living room floor, surrounded by papers.

'We must help her,' Amy said.

'In a moment,' Lydia replied, 'but first have a look at some of those papers. She won't see you.'

Amy stepped forward gingerly and gazed at the mass of correspondence. There were credit card statements, bank statements, store card statements, mortgage statements, statements that seemed to vie with each other for importance. And scores of letters. Amy turned one over to see that it was from a debt collection agency threatening to send bailiffs to 'seize your goods'. There were dozens that began, 'We are most disappointed that we have not received a reply to our last letter . . .' There were blue bills, red bills, bills with underlining, bills with 'final warning' stamped across them. And there was one piece of paper with the crest of a court on it. And in the midst of all the threats one that started, 'You have been selected for our special low-rate loan . . .'

Amy looked back at Lydia. 'She reminds me of myself.'

'I know. I saw you cry like that.'

'But . . . how?'

'Never mind. What do you think her greatest need is?'

'For money to pay all these debts.'

'Perhaps,' Lydia said, 'although I doubt she will ever have enough money for that.'

'Has she been very foolish with money?' Amy asked.

Lydia's jaw hardened and for a moment Amy felt afraid of her. 'Yes, a little, but she hasn't been living extravagantly. She's been trying to be a good mother – one who wanted her kids to have a decent coat, and money for school trips, and presents at birthdays. Frank, her husband, was made redundant six months ago – he's out trying to find work now. This couple has often gone hungry so their kids could eat.'

'You make it sound like Dickens' time.'

'My dear, some people today are poor. They're not poor because they spend too much; they are just poor. They don't need a clever talk on how to make five meals out of two chicken bones. They need more income. She borrowed to live.'

'But she has a colour television and a video . . .' As soon as Amy said it, she regretted it. 'I'm sorry,' she added hastily.

'Good,' said Lydia, 'be sorry and realise that if you had four children – three of them under 10 – running around under your feet, *you'd* want a colour television and a video as well. Now, come on, what is this woman's greatest need?'

Amy shrugged.

'Amy, this is a most important lesson for you. Look at her. She's surrounded by paper – every piece of it screaming at her for attention. And that's not the half of it. There are the phone calls and the banging on the door. It's as if a whole world is saying "Pay me! Pay me!" . . . Her greatest need is for *hope*.'

Now it was Amy's turn to look annoyed. 'You make it sound so . . . emotional.'

'Debt *is* emotional, Amy,' Lydia replied. 'That's why you took the tablets. It's why people feel at their wits' end and why one debt expert suggested that over 70 per cent of couples who split up give money problems as their number one reason.[1] It's why mere "systems" of dealing with debt are never enough. We have to understand it: why we get into it, why it paralyses us, and yes, how – at its worst – it robs us of hope.'

'But even you have said she can never repay it all.'

'When you were small and you were afraid of the dark, what did your mother do?'

'She left the landing light on.'

'And that's what I'm about to do. I'm going to turn a light on for her. And you'll see that it will give her hope. And not just her, either; this light will even give her creditors – the people to whom she owes money – some hope of getting at least some of their money back. I must go back into the street for a moment, but please stay right where you are and listen to everything. Remember, she can't see or hear you.'

A moment later Amy heard the doorbell ring and watched as the woman got up, dried her eyes and went to answer it. When she came back into the room Lydia was with her. Amy went to say something and then realised that neither of them – not even Lydia – could see her.

'I came as quickly as I could,' Lydia was saying. 'I'm sorry you had to wait so long.'

'No, thank you for coming. The woman I met said that you would. My name is Sarah. Would you like a cup of tea?'

Lydia smiled at her. 'Hello, Sarah. I'm Lydia and, yes, I'm always ready for a cup of tea.'

PAY THEM FIRST

Sarah left the room and Amy could hear the sound of a kettle being filled. She watched as Lydia gazed at the mess of papers on the floor and then suddenly thrust open the window. Amy couldn't remember it being windy outside, but the second the window opened a huge gust came in and the papers began flying around the room. They swirled around her head, crashing into each other like a snowstorm with flakes the size of saucers. After a few seconds Lydia closed the window.

When Sarah came back with the tea most of the papers were piled up in what looked like a huge snowdrift in the far corner of the room. Only six letters and a court form remained on the carpet in front of the fireplace. 'What happened?' she said, looking around in surprise.

'Don't worry about that now,' said Lydia taking a cup from the tray. 'What pretty cups! I used to have a set just like this.'

Amy saw the same expression on Sarah's face that she imagined she herself had worn at the wishing well – a mixture of hopelessness, sheer relief and eyes that asked, "Who on earth *is* this woman?"'

Lydia sipped her tea and then put her cup down. 'Why were you crying, Sarah?'

'The debts,' Sarah said hesitantly. 'We've just lost control of them all. And if we go to prison, who will look after the kids?'

'Who told you you would go to prison?'

'Nobody . . . but one man rang four times last week and told my husband that our case was so serious it was being passed to a special debt agency. He suggested I sell my wedding ring to pay the money.'[2] Sarah started crying again.

Lydia took Sarah's hands in both her own. 'Listen to me very carefully. You are *not* going to prison. Have you ever seen a debtors' prison?'

'Only in *Oliver Twist*.'

'Exactly. That's because there aren't any. Now, would you mind picking up the six pieces of paper that are on the floor.'

'But what about all those stacked against the wall?'

'No, we'll look at those later. Just the six, please.'

The woman picked the bills up and gazed at them blankly.

'These are the ones that matter,' said Lydia. 'At the moment you are low on two resources: money and emotional strength. I see that all the time. Debt doesn't just rob us of money – it saps our will. This is a very important stage in getting out of debt – you have to first allocate what money you have and what emotional strength you possess to dealing with the most important debts.'

'But aren't they all important?'

'Yes, to the people to whom you owe the money they all matter, but to you and your family some are much more important than others.' Lydia took the six bills from her. 'It seems to me that out of all this paper only these need our attention straight away.'

'Why these six?'

'They're called "Priority Debts",' Lydia explained. 'If you are in financial trouble you should always deal with these first. Would you mind terribly going back to school for a moment?'

'I think I'd quite like it!'

'Well, it may be a bit simple, but I have this little device for remembering some of the priority debts. I call it "Pay T.H.E.M. F.I.R.S.T." – the letters all stand for one of the priority bills.

Tax (council)
Hire purchase
Electricity/gas
Maintenance and child support

Fines
Income tax
Rent/mortgage
Second mortgage
Television licence

' "T" is for tax – council tax. It's an important one because the council has a number of ways of recovering the money from you and in extreme cases they can ask a court to imprison you if you are in arrears.'

'We owe over a thousand pounds on council tax,' the woman said anxiously. 'But I thought you told me that people don't go to prison for debt these days?'

'I said there are no debtors' prisons now – and that's because hardly anyone goes to prison for debts other than for failing to pay fines. And in that case, imprisonment is really a result of the original criminal offence. The only debts you can conceivably go to prison for are not paying council tax (and then only if you are wilfully refusing to pay or have been "culpably negligent"), not paying any child support or maintenance orders, not paying income tax or national insurance contributions and not paying any court fines. And, of course, a fine is exactly what you're likely to get for not having a television licence – that's why it's on my list of priority debts.'

'What about all the others – credit cards, bank overdrafts, hire purchase, catalogue debt, store cards, mortgage arrears?'

'No – you can't be locked up for not paying those.[3]

I promise you we'll come back to them later, but let's look at the next one – "Hire purchase". The only reason this matters is because unlike buying something with a loan or on a credit card, with hire purchase your goods can be repossessed. If you've paid less than a third of the total amount owed, they don't even need a court order to do this.'

'Our washing machine is on hire purchase. It cost about £300 and we've paid just over £80.'

'Well, we'll need to do something about it, then – we don't want them taking that off you! The next ones are "Electricity" and "Gas". I see you have notices from both saying they're going to disconnect you.'

'Those are the biggest worry,' Sarah agreed with a shudder, 'those and the water rates – we owe them money too.'

'The water people can't disconnect you,' Lydia assured her, 'but we can't have you going without heat or light. The first of your debts we must do something about are your gas and electricity bills.'

'I'm trying to work out what the "M" is.'

'It stands for "Maintenance payments and child support".'

'Nothing owed there,' Sarah said.

'And "F" is for "Fines",' Lydia continued. 'Do you have any court fines?'

'The most we've had is a parking ticket and that was paid long ago.'

'Good, but if you did have some it would be important to contact the court and tell them you have trouble paying. They are normally understanding.'

'I promise you, Lydia, there are none.'

'Right, well, this may not take as long as I thought. The next one is "Income tax", which also includes things like national insurance contributions and VAT. If you don't pay those they could come and take some of your goods – even without a court order. I didn't see any papers from the Inland Revenue in the pile so I assume that isn't one you are bothered about?'

'No – all my tax comes out of my wages.'

'Then we're on to "R" for "Rent or mortgage" payments.'

Sarah had to swallow hard to keep from crying again. 'Well, this is our house, we bought it from the council ten years ago, but we've got a building society mortgage and we're three months behind with the payments. We just couldn't pay it and the credit cards and other loans.'

'It sounds to me as though you've been paying the wrong people first,' Lydia replied. 'Your mortgage is definitely another one that we have to deal with now. Let's keep going with those priority debts. "S" is for "Second mortgage". Do you have another mortgage as well as the one with the building society? Sometimes it's called a secured loan, a further advance or a second charge.'

'Yes – £10,000 with a company we saw advertised on the television.'

Amy saw Lydia's jaw tighten again. 'Right. Well, we'll deal with it,' she said firmly. 'And finally, "Television licence".'

'We've got another six months to run on that.'

'Good.' Lydia picked up her tea again, took a sip, and then spoke very deliberately. 'My dear, it would be foolish to tell you not to worry about your debts, but I will tell you this – don't waste a moment's worry on any of the debts piled up over there against the wall. Remember what I said earlier: "there is nothing they can do to you".'

Sarah nodded.

'The important thing now is to tackle the priority debts. Use all your efforts to deal with your mortgage, electricity, gas and council tax arrears first. Now, do you know how much money you have spare every month to make any payments towards these arrears?'

'I know it sounds silly, but I haven't got a clue and I don't think Frank would either. It comes in, we pay what we can and usually it's all gone at the end of the month.'

Lydia opened her bag and took out one of her "Reality Check" forms. Amy recognised it immediately. 'I know you don't want another piece of paper, but this one is a life-saver. It will help you know exactly where you are financially and later we'll use it to keep your creditors off your back.

'First put down any wages you get after deductions. Only include overtime if it's regular. Next, put in your child benefit and any other benefits you and Frank get, including any of those Frank gets because he's out of work.'

Lydia waited while Sarah filled in her income and then continued, 'Next we need to work out how much you have going out every month.'

'I'm not very good at maths. To be honest, figures scare me a bit.'

'I've heard that from a lot of people, Sarah, but it's not difficult. Just do it a line at a time.'

It took well over an hour to complete the spending part of the form. Sarah wasn't sure how much to put in for housekeeping and Lydia suggested £75 for a couple and £35 for each child. This included the kind of stuff you'd get in a normal supermarket shop – not just food, but toiletries, cleaning materials, bread and milk and small things you'd buy in between a supermarket shop.

There was space for things like birthday or Christmas presents, and "Emergencies" were for unexpected bills and repairs.

Clothing was estimated at £5 per person per week and Amy felt guilty when she recalled filling in her form and how much she had sometimes spent on clothes in a single Saturday afternoon.

When the form was completed Sarah went to make another cup of tea, and the second she left the room Lydia began sifting through the huge pile of papers against the far wall. When Sarah came back they were in seven piles.

Lydia was looking at the "Reality Check" form. 'Well, Sarah, after we've taken your spending away from your income, you have £80 a month left over with which to pay your creditors, and this is how we're going to use it. First we'll add £20 a month on top of your normal repayment to offer to your building society to repay your arrears and we'll offer £20 a month to repay your second mortgage arrears – we must protect your house at all costs.'

Sarah was writing it all down.

'Next, we'll write to the council and ask them to accept £10 a month towards the arrears on your council tax,' Lydia continued. 'Then we'll pay £10 extra on the hire purchase of the washing machine and finally we'll try to get an arrangement with the gas and electricity companies to accept a monthly amount of £5 each towards the arrears. That's a grand total of £70.'

Sarah looked dismayed. 'But that only leaves £10 a month to pay all the others.'

'Exactly,' said Lydia. 'There are seven other debts in all – water rates, credit cards, catalogues, a bank overdraft and a book club. We'll need to sort out your bank account and then you'll probably be able to offer a pound a month each to the rest.'

'They'll never accept that!'

'Sarah, whether they accept it or not – you simply *can't* pay any more. Unless you have a pile of money under your bed, it's all you can afford.'

'Perhaps they'll make us bankrupt.'

'I doubt it,' Lydia said firmly. 'Although it may not be such a bad thing as you think. Oh, I don't think for a minute that any of the people to whom you owe money will try to make you bankrupt, but you may decide to ask for it yourself.'

'Why on earth would I do that?'

'Because it would wipe off all your debts and give you a fresh start.'

'But they would take our house!'

'Not necessarily – it may well be possible for you to

keep your home. Anyway, that's for consideration later.'

'A pound a month seems so little. We never intended not to pay,' Sarah said quietly. 'I feel ashamed.'

'This way you *are* paying – you're paying what you can afford. And we'll keep it under review to see if there is any more spare when the other arrears are paid off.'

'I'm not sure we can get them all to accept that.'

'Well, we'll see, but let's try. And in any event I want you to make an appointment to see my friend Chloe – the one who sent me to you. She works at a debt counselling centre. There are places like it all over the country and some Citizens Advice Bureaux (CAB) also do this work. And they are free. Don't ever get debt advice from someone who wants you to pay them – perhaps taking a monthly percentage from your debt repayment for themselves. Remember, if an advice agency isn't free, be extra careful! They may be after what little money you've got left.

'Chloe will talk to you about your bank account – I can see from your bank statements that you are over your overdraft limit – but you must have an account to pay your wages into and from which to pay your creditors. She may suggest you open a new one – just a basic account with no overdraft facility – and we'll add your current bank to the people you'll be trying to pay over a period of time. Chloe will also write to all the people to whom you owe money and from then on they will deal with her. And heaven help them if they start to harass you when she gets involved!'

Sarah started to cry again but this time Amy could see that the tears were different. This was sheer relief. 'I don't know how to thank you.'

Lydia smiled as she left the house. 'Just remember, you have four brilliant kids, you and Frank are fantastic parents, and yes, you've made a few mistakes, but who hasn't? Remember to ring Chloe as soon as I've gone.'

Suddenly Amy heard the front door close and found herself standing with Lydia in the street outside.

'That was amazing!'

'Oh, we've only just started, my dear. Save words like "amazing" for when I show you the power of compound interest!'

'But Sarah looked so different at the end,' Amy persisted.

'Of course she did – because I turned a light on for her,' Lydia explained. 'Debt befuddles us, it confuses us, we can't see the wood for the trees. And it's scary not to know what's going to happen. I have little patience with people who play the system to avoid paying what they owe, but most people aren't like that. They want to pay, but they need some help in seeing what's possible. Just remember the basics: work out what you have coming in and work out what you have going out. Make sure you remember to pay THEM FIRST and then pay what you can – no matter how small it is. And get help. There are hundreds of people like Chloe – some are volunteers, some are lawyers, some work full-time and all of them do a fantastic job. In fact, I think you'd be brilliant at it. Here are some pay THEM FIRST notes. I'll put them in the biscuit tin together with a few jottings on bankruptcy.'

'It's just so sad.'

'It is sad, Amy,' said Lydia, 'but we're nowhere near finished and tomorrow we'll turn our attention again to your affairs! I want to talk to you about your "flexible friend".'

'Who's that?'

'Well, you're a little young to remember, but it was the name given to one of the very first credit cards in a famous advert. And with friends like this one, Amy, you have no need of enemies.'

6

A House of Cards

Amy was wise enough to have the kettle already
boiled by the time Lydia rang the bell, and within
minutes of arriving the older woman was sitting in the
one comfortable armchair, sipping tea. Amy was at
the table with a notepad in front of her. 'The next
class is on credit cards!' Lydia announced. 'The total
UK debt on credit cards exceeds £50 *billion*[1] and the
average adult in Britain now has personal debts of
£5,330 over and above any mortgage – much of it on
credit cards.[2] And when it comes to the plastic stuff
we really do lead Europe: nearly three-quarters of all

credit in Europe is taken up by the British![3] We now have 63 million credit cards in circulation – that's one for every man, woman and child in the country with a little to spare.'[4]

Amy was losing interest fast.

'Just figures, eh, Amy?' Lydia challenged. 'Well, what about the case of Stephen Lewis who earned £22,000 as a production worker and killed himself after running up a debt of £70,000 on nineteen different credit cards? His wife and family are still being pursued by some of the lenders.'[5]

'That was harsh,' said Amy. 'I know better than anybody how he felt.'

'I know you do, but I want you never to forget that feeling. Those who offer us credit spend millions of pounds on adverts that suggest that it's all sweetness and light – a real fun trip to borrow money. But why do you think the Chief Executive of the bank that owns the largest UK credit card company said recently, "I don't borrow money on credit cards and I tell my children not to. It's too expensive"?'[6]

'But in the book on financial management it said

credit cards were good if you pay off the balance at the end of every . . .'

'I know what they say,' Lydia broke in, 'but I want to show you why many financially astute people don't have credit cards at all and why it's vital not to have them if you are struggling to get out of debt. First, I agree with the Executive Director of that major bank (and I applaud his honesty) – they are too expensive. Second, when we use credit cards we spend more – one expert suggested up to 34 per cent more!'[7]

'But why is that?'

'Because they whisper to us, "This isn't *real* money." And I believe it's the reason that unless you've got a will of iron, it's best not to have a credit card at all. Credit cards pander to that characteristic we just looked at – impulse buying. Plastic makes it easier to miss out two crucial stages of purchasing something: "***Do I need it?***" and "***Can I afford it?***" '

'I don't suppose you can blame the shops for that.'

'No, you can't, but we don't have to make it easier for them! Impulse buying is much harder when you're limited by how much money you actually have in your bank account – and especially if you're limited by *how much cash you have on you*. But credit cards allow us to impulse buy till the cows come home. When did you last go to the cinema, Amy?'

'Last week. Why?'

'How did you book the tickets?'

'Over the telephone.'

'Very convenient – and when you got to the cinema you put your credit card in a machine and your tickets came out?'

'Well, yes, of course.'

'How much did they cost?'

'£14.50 – that's £6.25 each for my friend and me, plus a £2 booking fee.'

'When you bought them, how much money did you have in your ordinary bank account?'

'None – I was overdrawn.'

'So you had no money to go to the cinema, and decided to go to a money lender and borrow it at 19 per cent interest per year.'

'Well, if you put it like that – yes. But why are you saying 19 per cent? I don't think my rate is anything like as high as that.'

'I assure you it is,' said Lydia, pointing out the figure on the credit card statement.

'But I remember the advert when I took out the card. It said the rate would be less than 10 per cent – that's why I did it.'

'Don't be too hard on yourself; more than three-quarters of credit card holders don't know how much interest they are paying.[8] And, anyway, some credit card companies are magicians – they make your money disappear! One of their favourite tricks is the illusion of the "teaser rate". In this trick the magician runs huge advertising campaigns which show low annual interest rates. The rate looks very attractive but in reality only one in ten people get the cheap deals.[9] One banking insider said that consumers are being "duped" by banks offering these headline rates.'[10]

Amy sighed, and Lydia went on, 'And when your credit card bill comes, how much of it will you repay?'

'Well, I've always got a fair bit owing so it's never just the £5 – it's normally 3 per cent – the minimum. I do that every month.'

Lydia walked through to the kitchen. 'And how long do you think it will take you to repay those cinema tickets?' she asked, coming back with a calculator.

'I expect it's something silly like a year!'

Lydia had already started tapping. 'If only – fifteen years would be closer![11] And for every 180 months of those fifteen years, your money lender – the credit card company – will be adding on 19 per cent per year interest. And in addition to that they'll be adding on 19 per cent per year interest on the interest already built up!'

'You're right, Lydia, I know it,' Amy sighed. 'Using credit cards made it too easy for me to buy things I didn't need and didn't really even want. The thing is, though, all my friends got one as soon as we left school and they use them all the time.[12] It would just seem so unsophisticated not to have one. And if you do pay it off every month, it means that you've gained a bit of free credit.'

Lydia shook her head. 'No – that won't wash. First of all you'll only gain something if you have that money invested, or if you would have paid it from an overdraft. For most mortals, the slight monetary advantage you gain in not paying until the end of the month – say £5 on purchases of £500 – is chicken-feed compared to the disadvantage in terms of encouraging impulse buying. The truth is that the "pay at the end of each month" argument is one thrown about by the credit card industry because they know that only about 50 per cent of people actually do.'[13]

'What about sales?' Amy asked. 'Sometimes my credit cards have saved me money because they meant I could take advantage of sales – sometimes I saved up to 40 per cent.'

'It's not a saving of 40 per cent when you buy something that you would have done without if you didn't have a credit card. It's a loss of 100 per cent – and that's when you pay the balance off! If you don't, well, you've got interest on top as well . . .' Lydia broke off the sentence. 'Can you think of any more reasons to have a card?'

'Emergencies,' Amy replied promptly.

'I can't tell you how many times I've heard people use that one,' Lydia said, scowling. 'Amy, you don't need a credit card for emergencies – it's another one of the arguments that credit card companies trot out.

For someone with a debt problem, keeping a credit card for emergencies is like keeping a small nuclear device in your house just in case you are burgled! I concede that a credit card may be helpful for someone who jets around the world spending large amounts of money, but for most people a debit card – one that lets you use the money you have in your bank account – is perfectly adequate. And if you really do want to have a cushion you should arrange a modest overdraft facility on your bank account that you *only* use in emergencies.'

Amy had almost run out of arguments, but as she thought about how she handled her money another one struck her: 'But, Lydia, credit cards are so convenient.'

Lydia nodded vigorously. 'Now on that score, Amy, I have to agree with you. Credit cards are the most convenient way in the world of getting rid of money. Have you ever seen somebody drop 50p in a shop? They'll search high and low for it, other customers will join in as well and eventually someone will find it, hold it aloft and they'll all congratulate each other. But those same people who scoured the shop for 50p will hardly give a second look at an interest charge of £15 on their credit card statement, or at a late payment fee of £20. It seems that forty 50p's on a credit card statement aren't worth bothering about. Now that's convenient!'

They had lunch together and then Lydia said that she was tired. She closed her eyes and was soon fast asleep. Amy put a blanket around her and waited.

DEBT IN THE POST

It was a good hour later when Lydia stirred. 'How silly of me,' she said, looking at her watch. 'We don't have time for me to take naps – you should have woken me.'

'I've been in debt for years,' Amy said, laughing. 'Another hour's not going to make much difference. And, anyway, it gave me time to think. I wonder if you're being a bit unfair. You seem to have a bee in your bonnet about credit cards.'

Lydia's glasses had slipped off her nose as she slept and she searched under the cushions of the armchair as she replied, 'Amy, if people are comfortable with having them and paying them off at the end of every month, then I'd be the last to interfere – well, perhaps not quite the last! But what really makes me angry is the way that successive governments have passively allowed credit card providers to deceive, trap and exploit people. Just the other day an elderly man came to see Chloe at the debt counselling centre. His wife was disabled, he was on benefits, and he was beside himself with worry. He had debts of over £10,000, almost all of them built up on credit cards, and no real prospect of being able to repay them unless he sold his home.

'Chloe asked him how so much debt had built up and he told her he didn't know. He hadn't bought a new car or anything. He just kept getting credit card application forms sent to him and it got out of control. When he came in that day he'd only just realised he had no way of paying them back. He hadn't even told his wife.'

'But he needn't have taken all those cards on,' Amy said.

'Of course not, but as a nation we're incredibly under-educated with regard to credit cards. When we're offered a card, we somehow assume that because a bank is behind it, it's all right to borrow the money – otherwise they wouldn't lend it to us. But many banks have long since lost the sense of duty they used to have in looking after their customers. And one of the duties they've forgotten is to be responsible in lending.'

'They upped my credit limit without even asking me,' Amy put in.

'Well, that's an example of what I mean. Households in financial difficulties are *more* likely to have had their credit limit increased in the past twelve months than other cardholders. Some credit-risk managers in credit card companies have acknowledged that they raise credit limits in the knowledge that the highest-risk customers are also the ones that need and will use the increase.[14] I'm afraid that grabbing market share has clouded their judgment. If you've got a few hours to spare on the internet, it's not at all difficult to obtain five or six different credit cards with total credit facilities in the tens of thousands. Some credit card providers even target those with poor credit ratings for new business!'

If she'd heard it from someone else, Amy would

have been sceptical, but coming from Lydia she had no doubt it was true. She could only ask why. Why would credit card companies deliberately target those who were least able to afford to use them?

Fortified by a cup of tea and a couple of digestives, Lydia explained that credit card users are split between those who normally pay the balance off at the end of every month – 'convenience users' – and those sometimes called 'revolvers'. 'Revolvers' have certain characteristics: they make only minimum payments, they often pay late and even miss payments completely. Rather than hating the 'revolvers' the credit card companies grew to love them. 'Revolvers' make it easy to make healthy profits. And so they began to actively look for these characters – offering inducements on transferred balances and lowering minimum payments. And they found a prime source was in those with a poor credit rating. Many 'revolvers' have no idea how much they owe.

As she thought about what Lydia had said, it didn't take Amy long to decide that she was firmly in the 'revolver' category. 'The not really knowing how much you owe is one of the worst things,' she said. 'I think that's why debt pushes so many people to the edge. It's not just the fact that you owe people money – it's the worry. It somehow takes over your mind and robs you of the ability to think clearly.'

'I agree absolutely,' Lydia replied. 'And, in truth, all kinds of people are affected like that. After Stephen Lewis' death, his Member of Parliament, John Mann, took up his case. The MP has been inundated with letters from people in similar situations: mothers whose children have had to abandon university to pay their store card debts and pensioners who have been given credit of £90,000 on dozens of cards. One woman wrote, "I have spent the last five years robbing Peter to pay Paul until the debt escalated out of control. During that time, both NatWest and the Alliance & Leicester lent me further funds without checking my capacity to pay. I am currently in debt to the tune of £110,000." [15]

Lydia started rifling through her handbag yet again and the tension broke a little as Amy laughed at her. 'How many more bits of paper have you got in there?'

Lydia smiled. 'Here it is. It's a mail-shot from a

credit card company and I kept it especially. I've changed the recipient's name, but that's all. Read it out, will you?'

Amy took the letter:

Dear Mr Cartwright

Congratulations! This special notice confirms that you have been pre-selected to apply for a Capital One MasterCard with the following features:

- *Credit limit between £200 and £2,500*
- *Low monthly payments*
- *Choice of credit card designs*
- *A chance to build your credit history . . .*

'In other words,' Amy broke off from reading, 'they know this is someone who doesn't have a good credit history.'

'You're catching on fast,' said Lydia. 'Keep reading.'

Place the sticker of your preferred credit card design on your ultra short application form . . .

the convenience and spending power of a Capital One MasterCard can be yours free of charge.

'It's another one of those "free offers" that's too expensive!' Lydia said. 'And if Mr Cartwright is foolish enough to take their advice and apply for this card, it will turn out to be very expensive indeed. The annual percentage rate (APR) – which in essence means the *real* interest rate – on most credit cards is between 13 per cent and 20 per cent. This particular one is between 29.9 and 34.6 per cent!'

'It's outrageous!' Amy said. 'Completely outrageous!'

'Yes, it is. But what's even more outrageous is that successive governments – who rightly feel it their duty to protect us in hundreds of different ways – seem to totally lose their nerve when it comes to financial institutions. They allow the most vulnerable to be preyed upon by the very strongest.' Lydia tucked her legs underneath her and leaned back comfortably on the sofa. 'Do you want to hear something else that's incredible about the way they target customers?'

'Tell me,' Amy said settling back in her chair as well. Despite the seriousness of the subject, the warmth of their growing friendship was something she could enjoy.

WHEN PAYING ON TIME
ISN'T GOOD ENOUGH

'Lenders may well turn down your application for a card if your credit rating is too good!'

'Explain, please,' Amy asked the older woman, not bothering to register her surprise – she was becoming used to the unbelievable.

'There was an article about it in the papers the other day – "*You're just too good for American Express Credit*". It was about a man who had been turned down by American Express because his credit history showed he was too good at paying his bills. As I just said, the lenders want customers who make money for them – in other words, the people who will get into debt and have to pay interest.'[16]

Amy thought how crazy it all was and then a question occurred to her. 'Lydia, I got a letter from one card company offering to transfer all my balances to their card and saying they wouldn't charge me any interest for six months – not even on new purchases. Surely that's a genuinely good offer?'

'Don't be so sure. Would you be able to pay the balance off in six months?'

Amy made a face. 'No chance – it would be way too big.'

'So what rate of interest would be charged once the six months' free period was over?'

'I'm not sure . . .' Amy said, looking downcast. 'I'm not very good at all this, am I?'

'Don't be too hard on yourself – a recent Treasury select committee had to ask a maths professor for help because it was struggling to understand the tariffs and charges published by high street card providers![17] But I'm not going to let you off the hook completely, Amy. Look, if you wanted to take a taxi to London – that's over fifty miles from here – you'd ask the driver for an indication of what the fare would be, wouldn't you?'

'Of course,' Amy agreed.

'And what would you say if he told you that the

first twenty-five miles were free?'

'I'd ask him what rate he'd charge *after* twenty-five miles.'

'And what if he told you that he'd set any rate he wanted after twenty-five miles?'

'I'd laugh at him and walk away,' Amy said.

'Exactly! And that's what I want you to do the next time a credit card company offers to do something for you for nothing!'

SOME PLASTIC SURGERY

Lydia was silent for a while and Amy sensed that something important was about to happen. She wasn't disappointed.

'Lay all your credit cards out on the coffee table,' Lydia requested. Opening her purse, Amy unzipped the back section where she kept the cards and placed them on the table one by one – two blue, two gold, a grey and an orange one.

'Pretty, aren't they?' Lydia said with undisguised scorn. Eagle-eyed, she stopped Amy from zipping up her purse. 'What about those?'

'Oh, they aren't credit cards – just my Debenhams

store card and my Frasercard. I use them for buying clothes.'

'Put them on the table as well, but separate them from the credit cards. How much interest are you paying on them?'

Amy was puzzled. 'About the same as the credit cards, I suppose.'

'Wrong! No, Amy, when it comes to eating consumers alive, store cards are the kings of the jungle.' Lydia jabbed a finger at one of the cards. 'The rate on this one is 28 per cent a year, and on this little beauty . . .' Lydia picked the other one up, holding it outstretched between two fingers, as if she was afraid she might catch something nasty from it '. . . it is 29.3 per cent a year.'[18]

Amy's shock was visible. 'Why on earth did I . . . ? Of course, I took it out because the shop assistant said I could get a 10 per cent discount on the top I was buying.'

Lydia smiled. 'I'm sorry, Amy, but if that top cost £30, it means you got £3 off, right?'

'Yes,' Amy answered, feeling embarrassed already.

'And if you repay it at the 4 per cent minimum, let's

see how long it will take you to pay it off in full.' Lydia produced the calculator again. 'Fifteen years again! Which means the top will end up costing you . . . over £60.'[19] They both exploded with laughter.

'Amy,' Lydia began once she quietened down, 'when people use a store card they really believe they have a relationship with that store – Debenhams, House of Fraser, B&Q and so on – but it's quite likely they're actually in a relationship with a bank called GE Consumer Finance.

'GE operates over 50 per cent of the store cards in the UK. GE Capital, now GE Consumer Finance, set itself up in the 1930s *"to help our customers finance appliance purchases during the depth of the Depression"*. In other words, GE Capital was created to help people buy the products of its parent company, products people needed but couldn't afford. The modern GE Capital helps people to buy things from *other* companies that those customers often *can't* afford and often *don't* need. I believe that one of the strangest sights in the world must be that of people who consider themselves well-heeled, shopping in expensive shops and using a store card.'

'Well at least it's convenient!' Amy put in.

'You're getting the hang of this,' Lydia laughed. 'It is convenient – so much so that almost half of the people who take out credit in shops hadn't planned to do so when they left home.[20] The only problem is that the interest rate of most store cards (one exception being John Lewis) is four times the rate of some credit cards. A member of a Treasury select committee called the way they operate "highway robbery".[21]

'Now,' she continued, 'it's time for a little plastic surgery. Have you got a sharp pair of scissors?'

Amy knew without asking what Lydia expected her to do, but just as she was about to cut the first card in half, Lydia stopped her. 'Amy, I'm a bossy old woman, I know. I just want to make sure you are completely happy to do this – it's your choice, not mine.'

'I wish I'd done it years ago.'

The slaughter took just over a minute, and when it was over the table and floor were littered with plastic.

'Amy, you've just staged an incredible escape,' Lydia announced. 'It's not something everyone will be able to understand – only those who have been chained to debt know its incredible power – but today you've broken some of those chains. And the balance of power has shifted to you.'

'How can that be?'

'Because you have taken control. Up to now you've been trying to fight a monster that has been getting bigger every month by feeding off you. What you've just done is cut off its food supply. From now on the monster is going to get smaller.'

Amy took a deep breath in, hardly daring to believe it could be true, and before she could ask how it would happen Lydia went on to explain.

'I want you to use a technique that used to work for the smallest boy in my class when I was at primary school. Charlie was always getting bullied, until one day, out of sheer frustration, he took a swing at his tormentors and, as luck would have it, caught the biggest child in the class square on the jaw. The bully reeled, stumbled and fell . . . and Charlie never had to fight again. When you hit the biggest first – the others look after themselves.'

'But what's that got to do with my credit cards?'

'I want you to hit the biggest one first. Continue to

pay the minimum amount each month on all your credit cards *except* for the one with the highest rate of interest. Set your sights firmly on that one and pay as much money off it each month as you possibly can. Now that you've cut the card up, the debt isn't going to get any bigger, and after a while the balance will start to reel and one day it will fall to zero.'

Amy grabbed a pen and paper and starting making notes as quickly as she could.

'Once you've cleared the first card, start to attack the next most expensive card. Throw all the money you had been using to pay off the first card at it, plus the minimum repayment you were making anyway. Amy, it's amazing how fast those cards can fall.'

Amy was still scribbling as Lydia went off to fetch her coat. 'Make a list of all your cards with the amounts owed and the interest rates. We'll look at it tomorrow. I'll put a note for you in the biscuit tin.'

'Will do,' Amy agreed. 'And why don't I be clever and transfer as much as I can to a card with a "transfer your balance at 0 per cent for six months" offer?'

Lydia walked back into the room, her face looking distinctly cross. 'Amy, you have been addicted to credit. Do you think I am going to risk letting you have a card with a nil balance that you can start using again? Even if you *have* cut them in half! Many people who use the 0 per cent transfer deal end up with twice the debt! No, we'll avoid the temptation and forgo being clever. I'll see you tomorrow.'

'You will come back, won't you?'

'I will, as long as you promise not to glue those cards together!'

7

Stupid Alice

'Not a tube of glue in sight!' Amy said as she opened the door to Lydia the next day.

'Good!'

'But I do have a small question I'd like to ask you . . . now that my credit cards are gone, how do you suggest I pay for things?'

Lydia laughed. 'Amy, let me tell you one of my favourite stories. I heard it years ago from an old friend. It's called "The Wonder of Cash". Put your feet up and listen. I'll put the kettle on . . .'

The Wonder of Cash

Herbert lived in a small village. He worked as a farmhand and every week the farmer gave him £200 in wages. When he brought his money home each week, Herbert and Alice, his wife, would spread the cash out on the table in piles of £10. And then they would begin to plan how they would spend it. Alice had never passed an examination but she was nevertheless very good with money and she used what she called her cup bank. Every week she put different coloured cups on the table, each one carefully labelled.

First she would put £80 in the cup marked 'Rent'. The collector called every Saturday morning and he had never been disappointed. Next she put £60 in the cup marked 'Food'. There were cups for 'Gas', 'Electricity', 'Clothes', 'Insurance', 'Holidays', 'Council Tax' and a few others. When bills had to be paid monthly, or even yearly, Alice would work out how much they needed to put in the cup each week so that it would be enough by the time the payment was due. And finally Alice would put whatever was left in the 'Savings' cup. There was rarely more than £20 spare to put in there. Some weeks, she found there was more money than she needed in one of the cups, and when that happened she put it into her 'Rainy Day' teapot where it built up over the years.

It is true that Herbert and Alice had few luxuries, but if you had asked them whether they were poor, they would have smiled and said, 'Of course, not. We have a warm house, plenty of food, holidays, and we save a little.' And then they would have added, 'We don't have any debts.'

One day their next-door neighbour, Clarence, called in to see them. He was a foreman on a nearby farm and earned twice as much as Herbert. When he called, Herbert and Alice were dividing Herbert's wages up as they did every week, the cups lined up across the kitchen table. Clarence asked what was happening and when they told him he laughed out loud.

'You're so unsophisticated,' he exclaimed. 'And foolish! You shouldn't leave your precious money in those silly cups – it ought to be in a bank earning interest.'

Herbert felt stung that he and Alice had been so foolish. 'How much interest does your money earn, Clarence?' he asked.

'Two per cent!' Clarence replied proudly.

The next day Herbert met Clarence in the street and asked if he would help him look after his money in a better way. 'Delighted!' said Clarence. 'Meet me in the pub on Tuesday night!'

'But don't tell Alice,' Herbert urged.

'Mum's the word!' shouted Clarence, tapping his nose.

Herbert sat wide-eyed as Clarence explained what sophisticated people did with their money. He felt embarrassed that he had let Alice, who obviously didn't have a clue about finance, look after their affairs.

Clarence told him that clever people put all their money in a bank and then, instead of cash, the bank gave them a piece of plastic to use. It was practically magic. All the shops seemed to prefer it to cash, but if you ever needed any readies you could put the plastic in a hole in the wall and real money would come out. The bank paid you interest on any money you didn't use and it just built up and up.

It sounded too good to be true.

'Has anybody ever stolen your card, Clarence, and bought things for themselves using your money?'

'Yes, plenty of times. In fact, somebody once went to the trouble of actually making a card just like mine and using it. But it's no problem. You just tell the bank and they normally give you all the money back.'

'What do you mean by "normally",
Clarence?'

'Oh, don't worry about that.'

That night Herbert told Alice how he was
going to take charge of their financial affairs
from then on and, with the help of Clarence, get
a plastic card that could even give them money
from a hole in a wall. Alice had a dreadful
feeling that something was wrong but because
she knew that she wasn't clever she didn't argue.

Herbert couldn't wait for his first bank
statement to see how much interest his money
had made him, and when he heard the
postman come he rushed to the door, as he used
to do on his birthday when he was a boy.

When he saw the figure he couldn't believe it
– seven pence!! How could it possibly be true?

Alice, who was foolish with money, explained
it to him. 'We put £800 in over the month. All
our bills came out and just our savings stayed
in. On average we accumulated £3 a day

earning interest at 2 per cent per annum.'

'Well, it's better than nothing!' said Herbert, 'and better than it was just standing in those cups of yours!'

It was in the third month that things began to go terribly wrong. One day Herbert met Clarence in the street and said, 'Do you sometimes find that you spend more with the card than you used to with cash?'

'I can't remember the cash days, old boy!' Clarence answered. 'Don't worry about it!'

When the statement came at the end of the third month Herbert wasn't anything like as keen to rush to get it. In fact Alice opened it. Her face went pale. 'It says we've got minus £23 and somebody has taken £20 out of our account. There's a letter as well, but I don't understand it.'

Herbert snatched the statement from her and rushed around to Clarence's house. He caught his neighbour just as he was leaving for a darts match.

'What's happened to my money and who's taken that £20?'

Clarence told Herbert to calm down and explained. 'This month you somehow spent £23 more than you had in.'

'But how can I spend money I haven't got?' asked Herbert.

'Well, the bank allowed you to do it by lending you some of their money.'

'But I didn't ask to borrow their money.'

Clarence coughed. 'Well, that's the problem. I should probably have explained it to you. It happens to me all the time. Because you spent more than you had in, and you hadn't asked the bank to lend you the money, they lent it to you without asking you if you really wanted it. It's what they call an "unauthorised overdraft".'

'Did they want me to borrow it?' asked Herbert.

'No, they were very cross that you did.'

'Then why did they lend it to me?'

'Because you are a good customer,' said Clarence.

'And will they charge me interest?'

Clarence coughed again. 'Well, yes – rather a lot actually. In fact – 27 per cent.'

'And is that the £20 they've taken from my account?'

'Oh no, the interest charge will come next month. That £20 is for the letter they wrote to you telling you you've spent too much. If you don't put it right soon they'll send you another one and charge you again.'

Herbert walked home clutching the bank statement with his head held low. When he got in Alice was making their supper.

'Alice, I've been foolish,' he said. 'When you put our money in the cups every week we knew how much we had and what we had left. If we didn't have it, we didn't spend it. I felt silly that our money wasn't earning interest, but after just three months at 2 per cent we've only made *nineteen pence. And after one mistake, the bank has charged us £20 and next month they are going to charge us 27 per cent on the extra money we borrowed.'*

Alice smiled. 'Don't worry, Herbert,' she said. 'It's not your fault. We're just not clever enough to use our money wisely. Next week we'll go back to the cups.'

Herbert felt so relieved. In fact, that night at the pub, he told everybody he met what had happened and how only very clever people could handle their money wisely. He and Alice were going back to their silly cups. Word of stupid Alice and her cups spread like wildfire.

The next day when Alice opened the door to get the milk, there was a queue of people waiting to see her. She didn't know all of them but she did recognise the man from the library, the teacher and her butcher. The man in the very front had been there over an hour. He was the local solicitor. 'Are you Stupid Alice?' he asked.

> *'Yes,' she said, 'that's me.'*
>
> *'We were wondering if you could show us how to use the cups.'*

Amy chuckled as the story came to an end. 'And is that the answer to my question? Now that my credit cards are gone, you want me to use cash?'

'Only for a while, Amy. I'd be happy for you to use a debit card later, but I would like you to just use cash for three months. We've talked about being on a financial diet – well, this is the crash diet! It's only for those who want to get a real taste of what it's like to be out of debt for ever. For that to happen you have to believe again in the real value of money, and to achieve that there is nothing like real *cash!*'

'So, what do I do?'

'Every Monday I want you to go to the bank or cashpoint and take out the amount of cash you'll need to last you the whole week. In other words, you'll need to add up all the items in your budget that aren't paid directly from the bank by standing order or direct debit – things you would normally buy with your credit card or with cash such as food, newspapers, petrol, clothes and so on. And don't forget that you have a monthly budget, so after adding up all the cash items, you'll need to multiply by twelve and divide by fifty-two to get your weekly cash allowance.'

'Why can't I just get what I need every day from the hole in the wall?'

'Because, although they are very convenient, unfortunately, like credit cards, they whisper to us: "This isn't real money." They make it just too easy. Have you have heard the one about the man using a cashpoint machine? First he took out £10, then another £10, then £20, then £50. There was quite a queue building up behind him. Finally a man at the back lost patience and yelled, "Do you mind if we have a go?" The man at the machine shouted over his shoulder, "Not while I'm winning!" '

Amy pretended to ignore her and mumbled 'Cash!' under her breath, as if she was being asked to use some cranky new invention.

'Let me show you how it works,' Lydia said giving the younger woman a push. 'Up till now, when you've been shopping and have seen something you like, you simply paid for it using your credit card. Now you're using cash for the next three months, you're going to have to ask a question that almost every previous generation in the history of the world had to ask when they went shopping: "Have I got the money on me to pay for it?" '

'But I don't want to carry the whole week's cash with me all the time,' Amy said, still protesting.

'Of course not – so do you know what will happen? There will be times when you'll want to buy something but don't have the money on you to pay for it. When that occurs you'll have no choice but to go home, get some of that precious cash that has to last until the end of the week and make a trip back to the shop, or, just as likely, not bother to go back at all because by then you'll have cooled on the purchase anyway. Good old cash will rob you of the impulse.'

'Talking of robbing – what if I get mugged?'

'Amy, you've been getting mugged by your credit card company every month! At least this way the mugger won't charge you a fee if you don't have enough money on you to make it worth his while.'

8
Don't Trust Your Grandmother

It was four days since Amy had first met Lydia in the park, but already she felt as if she knew the older woman well. 'Thank you for spending all this time with me. I feel so very different.'

'I've enjoyed getting to know you, Amy, and you're proving a fast learner, but our time together isn't over yet. Tomorrow I'm going to show you debt at work in the lives of others – both the rich and the poor – and I tell you now that some of it is unspeakably sadder than you could possibly imagine. But today I want to show you a situation that you must never forget.'

'Is it the money secret?'

Lydia shook her head. 'No – not yet.'

They were standing together on a roof-top. The sounds of the city surrounded them and beneath them lay a huge shopping precinct. It was lunch-hour and thousands of office workers milled around the shops.

Amy looked down at the street below: 'They're buzzing around like flies.'

'Yes,' said Lydia, 'and one of them is about to meet the spider. Look closely at that young man on his mobile telephone.'

'Who is he talking to?'

'His bank.'

'You don't like banks, do you?'

'Amy, I have owed a great deal to banks – and not just money!'

'*You* have owed money?'

'Of course. There are things for which it's wise to borrow money; I call it "good debt". It may be finance for a house purchase, to start a business, or perhaps to buy a car that you need to do your job or to get your children to school every day. I've had some wonderful bank managers – people who cared about the businesses I ran, and one or two who actually cared about me as well. One of the most frustrating things in the business world is when the bank manager with whom you've built a good rapport moves on or retires.'

'I can't imagine you running a business,' Amy exclaimed.

'Why? Because I don't wear expensive clothes or drive a fancy car? Amy, I've gone past all of that. No, it's not that I don't like banks. But I have to say that I don't much like what many of them have become. Many people in banking – especially personal banking – tell me that over the past decade it has changed so much, with an incredible pressure on sales targets. And that brings us to one of the most sobering lessons we will look at together. If you want to be free of debt for ever you must constantly remember that no matter what people say, or how many letters they write to you congratulating you on the fact that "you have been selected for a loan", and no matter how many people tell you they have "just the product for you", you can't trust many of them.

Amy, what was the most frightening fairy tale you were told when you were small?'

'They were all pretty scary. Giants and beasts, poison apples and dwarfs, ugly sisters and wicked uncles.'

'Well, let me prompt you a little. What about "Little Red Riding Hood"?'

'That was the worst!' Amy agreed, giving a mock shudder.

'Can you think why?'

'Because the girl thought it was her grandmother in the bed, but really it was the wolf.'

'I believe it's the most terrifying story of all. You expect the giant to try to kill Jack, the ugly sisters to plot Cinderella's downfall, and the wicked witch to give a little trouble – but your own grandmother! If you can't trust her, who can you trust? Those who are in debt need impartial advice, and there is nothing worse than people taking advantage of them.'

'But does that really happen?'

'All the time. Just the other day Chloe had a client who had masses of credit card debt and a personal unsecured loan from his bank. He had a large mortgage on his house which he owned jointly with his wife, and went to see a financial advisor who suggested he take out a second mortgage to clear all the credit cards and the personal loan. The advisor said that this would mean he would only have to make a simple monthly payment which would be less than the total he had to pay out on the cards and the loan.'

'What was wrong with that?'

'Just about everything – a high interest rate on the second mortgage, fees for this, that and the other, a huge penalty for early repayment of the personal loan and, worst of all, he had been advised to pay off non-priority debts by mortgaging his house. In the event, the poor man couldn't keep the payments up and now, instead of the hassle of dealing with the credit card companies, he's facing losing his home.'

'What should he have done?'

'He simply needed to negotiate an arrangement with the credit card companies. If he had defaulted on the cards, the companies would have probably agreed to freeze the interest and let him pay the balance off at an affordable rate.'

'But why didn't the financial advisor tell him that?'

'Because he wanted the commission that the second mortgage company would pay him for the introduction,' Lydia said angrily. 'Let me tell you something else that happened to Chloe. A parent came to see her waving a letter his son had just had from a bank. The boy had been summoned to see his bank manager because he was overdrawn on his account. The father was glad; this boy needed some financial discipline from his bank. He looked forward to seeing his son suitably chastened. But when he asked how the interview had gone the boy said, "Pretty good, Dad. He gave me a £100 overdraft and a visa card!"

'The letter that the father brought in to Chloe stated the APR – the real yearly rate of interest – on the £100 overdraft. See if you can guess what it was? If you get it right in three, I'll buy you tea at the Ritz!'

Amy wondered if Lydia had ever had tea at the Ritz – the offer seemed to have slipped out rather easily. She started high: 'Twenty per cent!'

'Higher,' said Lydia.

'Twenty-five per cent!'

'Higher – and I have to tell you that at the moment you are nowhere near dining in one of the finest hotels in the world.'

Amy thought she had nothing to lose and blew the last guess extravagantly. 'Sixty per cent!'

'If only,' Lydia said grimly. 'No, my dear, this major bank gave a Visa card and an overdraft with an interest rate of over 111 per cent to the young man they should have been guiding and helping! And in case you don't believe me, here's part of the letter confirming the arrangement.'

INTEREST

Interest is payable at our Standard Personal Overdraft Rate (at present 1.45% per month, the APR is 111.7%). This APR, and the one quoted below, are calculated assuming you borrow the full £100 for a whole year and that the £5 monthly account operating charge is paid every month for a full 12 month period.

If you need a larger overdraft, please discuss this with us first, as if your borrowing exceeds an agreed limit, interest on the excess will be charged at our Unauthorised Overdraft Rate (at present 2.00% per month, APR 125.2%).[1]

Amy shook her head in disbelief as she read what the bank had written. 'But how can they do this?'

'Well, in order to get the overdraft the boy had to switch to an account with a monthly fee of £5 – which means that to get the £100 he has to spend £60 a year anyway – and with the normal overdraft interest the whole package came to that astonishing APR – 111 per cent. I don't know how they had the gall to put it in writing!'

'So the bank didn't help him at all?' Amy said, slapping the letter down on the table.

'Of course it didn't. But what's even more amazing is that they also got him to sign up to a Visa card!'

'But why – if he was such a bad financial risk?'

'Well, we talked about it a little earlier – sometimes banks target those with poor credit ratings and offer them cards with a very high interest rate saying that "it will help you rebuild your credit rating". But the second reason is that, these days, banks are like shops. It's just a little harder to see all the goods displayed but I assure you they are there: loans, credit cards, pension plans, fee-paying accounts, insurances. Your grandmother is into the retail business!'

Lydia turned her attention back to the young man with the mobile phone in the street below. 'Look at him. He thinks he's on the phone to his grandmother but he's about to see what big teeth she's got! Listen hard – can you hear the conversation?'[2]

'COME IN TO MY PARLOUR,' SAID THE SPIDER TO THE FLY . . .

Amy remembered thinking that if MI5 ever discovered Lydia, it would save them a fortune in listening devices. She could hear every word.

'I was wondering if I could increase my overdraft limit by £100?' the young man was saying. 'It's the end of the month and money's a little tight.'

'May I have your account number, please?'

'3-5-6-8-9-7-0-0.'

'Thank you. I see that you're actually due for an annual review anyway. Could you slip in to see us?'

*'Well, I'm on my lunch-hour now and I'm just
around the corner.'*

'Fine, come in straight away.'

Amy watched as the young man hurried along the
street and into the bank.

'Let's take a closer look,' said Lydia.

Amy found herself in an office – she had long since
stopped worrying about people seeing them, or even
how Lydia got them there in the first place. She
watched as a young woman, with a badge that read
'Sally Bowshaw: Personal Banker', got up from her
desk and went to greet the young man who was now
sitting rather nervously in the reception area. He
followed her into the office and sat down.

'Now, how can I help?' said Sally Bowshaw.

'Well, as I said on the telephone . . .'

*'I've been looking at your account and I can see
you've got a loan of £3,200 with us.'*

'Yes.'

*'Do you have any other loans with anybody
else?'*

'Yes, I've got one of £9,000 with a finance company for a car I bought two years ago.'

'And you are overdrawn by £300?'

The young man's head went down. 'Yes.'

'I see from your details that you earn £12,000 a year?'

'Yes.'

'I think we can help you.'

'Great!'

'What we'll do is this. We'll lend you £15,000 over seven years. That will allow you plenty to pay off both the loans and the overdraft and still have at least £1,500 spare. You might need it for a holiday or something.'

'Sounds wonderful!'

'And your repayments will still be slightly less than you are paying now!'

Amy turned to Lydia. 'That sounds pretty good to me.'

'It's not hard to reduce somebody's monthly repayments when you extend the payment time by 40 per cent!' Lydia snorted. 'But watch closely, here comes the first sting.'

'Now the rate of interest on this special loan is only available to our Premium Plus account holders,' Sally Bowshaw was explaining to her client. *'You pay just £10 a month for that, but you get free travel insurance. Do you go abroad much?'*

'No, I can't afford to.'

'Well . . . there are lots of other benefits and it will get you our special loan rate.'

Amy turned to Lydia. 'Explain, please.'

Lydia scowled. 'This young man doesn't need a Premium Plus account or even a special silver account or a platinum-coated account. He needs, and qualifies for, free banking. But he hardly knows what's going on . . .' She broke off to listen to what was happening. 'Wait for it, Amy, he's about to be hit by sting number two – the "Nomad in the Sahara Umbrella Trick".'

'Whatever's that?' Amy whispered, trying to listen to the banker at the same time.

'You sell somebody something they've never seen before, can't afford and will probably never use. Keep watching!'

The personal banker smiled. 'Now I expect you'll want some insurance protection in case you're ever unable to work. That will cost £3,500 payable monthly over the seven years.'

Lydia sighed so loudly that Amy thought the personal banker was sure to have heard her. 'Insurance to cover the monthly payments on loans and credit cards is one of the great scams.' It was the nearest Amy had heard Lydia get to swearing.

'Sometimes it's called Payment Protection Insurance, but actually it means Pretty Pathetic Investment. It is meant to provide peace of mind by covering your repayments in case of illness, unemployment or accident. It is over-priced and so complicated that nobody other than a specialist could possibly understand it. One such specialist put it like this: "I've worked in this industry for eleven years, yet I've never bought a single policy – and I'd recommend you do the same." '[3]

'You really are getting steamed up,' Amy laughed.

'I'm sorry, Amy, but I feel so strongly about it. Why, just the other day in Parliament an MP raised the case of one of his constituents who had been sold Payment Protection Insurance adding an extra £1,000 to the loans she had taken out for her daughter's wedding. The only problem was that Payment Protection Insurance is to guard against losing your job – and this woman was unemployed! I can tell you that one day banks are going to face massive claims for many of these wrongly sold policies.'[4]

'But why do the banks try to sell it so strongly?'

'Well, one reason is that it's an "add-on" – like trying to sell you a tie after you've bought a shirt. And if that was *all* it was you could understand it, but there's a more sinister reason that has little to do with wanting you to be protected.'

Lydia went on to explain that banks must always quote the APR on loans and that naturally there is tremendous competition between them to show it as low as possible. Because Payment Protection plans are not a *compulsory* part of the loan agreement, however, they can be left out of the calculation that decides the APR.

'Of course,' she added, 'some insurance protection can be wise, but some banks sell it indiscriminately. I would always recommend people not to take it out at the same time as the loan but if they want it, to shop around for the very best deal, and get advice from somebody independent.'

They turned their attention back to the young man. His personal banker was just finishing.

'There – all your loans paid off, and one man-ageable monthly repayment!'

Lydia snorted. 'It reminds me of the bank advert I once saw that said, "Now you can borrow enough from us to get completely out of debt." Look at the form he's about to sign. Can you see the figure at the bottom of it?'

Amy gasped. 'With interest he'll be paying back £22,810.10 over seven years!'

'Yes, and it all started with a phone call to increase his overdraft by £100. Wasn't he lucky that it was time for his annual review! The good thing about some banks is that they don't let things like calendars get in the way of annual reviews – you can have as many a year as you like.'

'But can he afford the loan?'

'Of course not! What's likely to happen is that in a year or so's time he will need to take out a new loan and spread that over an even longer period. He's 22 years old, he may want to get married some day, but now he'll have a huge loan around his neck until he's almost 30.'

'Do you think this kind of thing is common?'

'It's not only common, it's the way many banks operate these days. It's absolutely normal. Every customer is a potential target for sales. It could be anything from accounts that carry a monthly fee, new loans, credit cards or insurance. Every sales person has a target sales figure.'

'Isn't that what happens in every business?' Amy asked, trying to be fair.

'Yes, it does,' Lydia agreed, 'but in banking there's a difference – or at least there should be. Do you remember why I said that Red Riding Hood was such a terrifying story?'

'Because the girl thought she was talking to her grandmother.'

'Exactly. When people deal with their bank many of

them think it is still the same institution it always used to be. If you say the word "bank" to most people the associations are of stability and integrity – we think of banks as part of the "system", almost like the police or the local town hall. But the past twenty years have seen massive changes in the way banks operate. And with some banks, your grandmother has become the wolf, but you don't know it. It's as if your doctor, who used to be so careful in giving out prescriptions, has suddenly changed character, done a deal with the drug companies and is now dispensing tablets as though they were going out of fashion. But you still trust him and so you take every one of them.'

'But what can be done?'

'Only one of three things. Either banks will change – and they may well do so: maybe an enlightened government will make them – or perhaps they'll realise that just like the financial services industry with the endowment mortgage scandal, one day they will have to give an account of all this advice – after all, they portray themselves as trusted advisors.'

'What's the other possibility?'

'That Red Riding Hood gets herself a little education

which will allow her to spot the difference between molars and fangs. The really sad thing is that so many people in the banking industry know what is going on and they don't like it. They actually want to give people good advice and be trusted again.'

The young man was now in the street and on his mobile phone again. He was talking to his best friend. 'My bank was brilliant. I can go on that holiday after all . . .'

'Bless his heart!' said Lydia.

9
Debt at the Door

On the fifth day Lydia asked if they could meet a little earlier than normal. It was only just after eight when Amy heard the bell ring. She welcomed Lydia in and offered her some tea.

'No – not even for me, just now,' Lydia said. 'Today we have so much to see and I'm sorry that you will witness some great sadness. First of all, we'll go somewhere where there are few credit cards, almost no bank overdrafts, hardly a store card in sight – and unbelievable debt. You are unlikely to ever face what these people have to deal with, but if you are to understand debt, you must see this side of it at least once.'

It was raining when they got there. The vast housing estate sprawled out at the edge of the city. The two women stood on top of a hill and looked down on row upon row of terraced houses. Amy thought Lydia looked sadder than she had ever seen her; the older lady was gazing into the far distance.

'A penny for your thoughts, Lydia.'

'Oh, it always moves me when I bring somebody here.'

'Do you mean to tell me that you've done all this with other people as well as me?'

'Hundreds, my dear: teachers and postal workers, plumbers and doctors, members of parliament and, on two occasions, financial advisors – debt is no respecter of persons.'

Amy was silent for a while and then asked, 'And why so sad here in particular – especially after all we've seen already?'

'You know, Amy, life wasn't always so hard in these parts. The time was when this area thrived with shipping and mining, but those days are long since gone; many of the people living here are now on benefit. It's no surprise that debt is a major problem here. Those on low incomes are three times more likely than the general population to be in arrears with rent, council tax, utility bills or mortgage.[1] Here are some of the very poorest and most vulnerable people, and yet, on this estate, we will find the highest interest rates and the deepest abuses. The average weekly income here is £200 and almost a third of it goes to pay door-to-door credit companies. Last year people in these three streets alone paid £374,000 to money lenders. Sometimes the APR on those loans reached 500 per cent.'

'But there have always been loan sharks.'

'Amy, it's not helpful to call them that. The vast majority of these loans weren't from shady individuals with dark glasses and Rottweilers, but from companies allowed to operate within the law by successive governments, the largest of which made pre-tax profits of £150 million in 2001.[2]

'Anyway, that's enough of numbers, it's time for you to see how it all works.' Lydia began striding down the hill towards the terrace of houses. She stopped outside Number 3, Jasmine Street.

'Pat Clancey lives here. She has two children, the oldest of whom has a severe learning disability, and she is totally dependent on benefit payments. In September two years ago her washing machine broke down and she borrowed £100 from a door-to-door cheque company to pay for a second-hand replacement. She was told by the man who arranged the loan on her doorstep that she would have to make repayments of £3 a week over fifty-three weeks. That is an APR of just under 164 per cent.[3]

'The following December, the door-to-door credit collector asked if she would like a little help with Christmas money. She borrowed another £200 and this time was given thirty-one weeks to pay it back at a rate of £10 per week. The APR on that loan was 365 per cent![4] By March of the next year she was a month in arrears on both loans, owing almost £50 in back payments. She was lent another £100, but the arrears were immediately taken from this and she was left with £50 in cash and a new weekly payment of £22 in total. Some weeks she goes without food to make the payments.'

Lydia grabbed Amy's hand and practically dragged her two doors down to Number 7.

'This is Albert Harries' home. He is 55 years old and a factory worker. He saw an advert run by a company that read: "*We understand that your pay-cheque sometimes doesn't go far enough. Whether you have received unexpected bills, spent more than you thought or just fancy a big night out before payday, we are here to help.*" He borrowed £400 and had to repay £500 at an APR of 1,355 per cent![5] When the loan company's Head of Customer Services was challenged by a journalist she said, "We don't like quoting APRs as they take a lot of calculating." [6]

Lydia turned away from the small house and they walked up the street together in silence. Amy spoke first. 'I had no idea that people lived like this. But why do they borrow money from such places?'

'Because they have little choice,' Lydia replied. 'It's the very poorest that need most help, but, ironically, it's the poor that end up paying more for everything.

More than half of households with serious debt are in the lowest income group.[7]

'Even household goods cost so much more. I could take you to one furniture chain which operates in areas where almost everybody is on benefit. They sell household items with advertisements such as "Only £4.99 a week!" The only problem is that a television that will cost you £264.99 in Argos will cost you £778.44 from this particular chain. This includes "service cover" at an incredible £273. A cooker worth £330 costs £934 if you pay for it over three years.[8] Or I could show you a shop where all the prices are quoted at the per-week hire purchase price in bold letters. The total cash price is in small letters underneath because people don't come into these shops to pay cash, and the interest rate (APR) can be almost 30 per cent!'[9]

'It's simply wrong,' said Amy.

'And these are the shops available to the poorest among us. Anyway,' Lydia said with an attempt at a smile, 'in the midst of all this despair there is *one* oasis. It's time you met Tom, the director of the local credit union.'

ANOTHER WAY

Hartvale Credit Union was nestled between the Spar and a kebab shop. 'I've never even heard of a credit union,' Amy said as she followed Lydia inside.

'Most people haven't, but that's only because in this country we're behind the times. In America a good part of the lending comes from credit unions like this one. They are non-profit organisations and lend to the community at a fraction of the cost of other lenders. And Tom Boston, the local director, is one of the best.'

Tom greeted the older woman as if she were his grandmother. 'It's good to see you! I've missed you.'

'Good to see you, too, Tom. Now do me a favour and explain to my friend here what you do.'

'Essentially, we encourage people to save with us. It's often quite small amounts, but when they've shown they can save for eight weeks they are eligible for a loan. A £100 loan from us would cost £3 in interest over a twenty-week period compared to £47 from a door-to-door lender.'

'But why doesn't everybody use you instead of

those companies that I've just heard about?' Amy burst out impatiently.

'Credit unions have been around for a long time, but until now we've been quite small and not very well known,' Tom explained. 'We're increasing in number quite fast, though, and there are now credit unions in many localities with local businesses and some banks providing capital that we can lend. It's always worth people trying to find a credit union near them. We can revolutionise the way they borrow money.'

Lydia interrupted, 'Tom, we have to be going soon, but could you just tell Amy what you feel about the door-to-door lenders?'

'Well, first of all, to be fair, you have to remember that they are often lending over short periods of time and that makes the APRs look very high indeed. If somebody lent you £20 and asked for £25 back in a month's time, it may not seem too bad – but it's actually an APR of 1,355 per cent![10]

'But even then, if people were just taking the loan as a one-off transaction, it wouldn't be so much of a problem,' Tom continued. 'The real difficulty with these lenders is the way they try to keep the borrowing going by constantly offering new loans – sometimes to allow the borrowers to make payments that are owed on *old* loans – and that, of course, means that there's always long-term borrowing going on at very high rates.'

'But how do they justify it?' Amy said.

'Basically in two ways,' Tom replied. 'First, they say they offer a personal collection service – something which people do like – and that is expensive to run. Second, they build into their rates the fact that people will probably miss payments occasionally without penalty. You can't hide behind the settee from a direct debit, but you *can* avoid the man who calls on a Friday night!

'They say that customer surveys show high levels of satisfaction,' Tom added frankly, 'but I ask, "Satisfaction with what?" Who in their right minds could be satisfied with sky-high interest rates? No, when people say they are satisfied, they normally mean that the collectors who call are usually friendly and efficient – and often people that they know. That's why it's so hard to default. In some ways I don't blame the companies, but what I do find staggering is that successive governments have let them get away with it for so long.'

'So why have they?' Amy asked.

'Now that really is a big question!' said Lydia before Tom could answer. 'Other countries have capped excessive interest rates, but not here. Here we allow the most vulnerable to be preyed on the most easily.[11] But there are some compensations – you don't worry about interest rates going up a quarter of a per cent when you're already paying an APR of 500 per cent!'

The two women said goodbye to Tom and set off along the road together. Lydia spoke first. 'Remember, Amy, we haven't even looked at the real loan sharks with their threats of violence and the like. I suppose they will always be with us, but I wanted to show you what we allow *within* the law. But now we're getting very near the moment you've waited for. It's not long now before we find the secret.'

'Where are we going?' Amy asked.

'Back to the docklands, but this time we're going to visit a home on the other side of the road. It's an apartment – the penthouse, in fact!' And with that

Lydia lengthened her stride until she got faster and faster and became a blur against the walls of the terraced houses. And just before she disappeared completely, she shouted over her shoulder, 'Do keep up!'

10

The Wealthy Pauper

Amy gazed out of the apartment window to the road below. In the distance she could see the old part of the docklands they had visited so recently. She even thought she could pick out Sarah and Frank's house, but now they were well and truly on the other side of the street.

The penthouse suite was the first to be sold when the apartments at Alexander Court went on the market, and looking around the huge living area Amy could understand why. The finishes were exquisite and the sheer expanse of wood flooring gave it an incredible sense of space. But without doubt it was their position that made these waterside apartments special – the views across the bay were fantastic. Without thinking what she was doing, Amy walked across the lounge, slid open the balcony doors and immediately heard the clattering of the sail ropes against the masts of the small yachts moored just underneath. If I lived here, she thought, I'd think I was permanently on holiday. She turned back to Lydia. 'Who lives here?'

'A man I call "the wealthy pauper".'

Amy laughed. 'What on earth is a . . . ?'

'Amy, debt is no respecter of income. Some people don't have *enough* income – they are simply too poor – and some of them live to the left of this road, but for most people the problem is not income, but *expenditure.*

'Many people on very small incomes live all their lives debt free, but remember what you learnt on the very first day: most of us spend about 10 per cent more than we earn – whatever that is. That's why salary rises fool people. They say, "Next January, when I have more income, we'll be fine." And they *are* fine for a while, but by May things are as bad as ever, or even worse. Sometimes they take drastic measures such as moving from a large house to a small one. For a while they have money in the bank and lower mortgage repayments, but within a year or two they are back in the same old state. Amy, this is one of the biggest lessons in escaping the scourge of debt: *unless you deal with expenditure you will never earn enough money to be debt free.*'

'What if you're a millionaire?' laughed Amy.

'Especially if you're a millionaire,' Lydia replied promptly. 'Come on – let's go and see our wealthy pauper.'

They went back through to the lounge. Amy jumped when she saw a young man sitting at a desk, and it took a few seconds for her to remember that she and Lydia were invisible to him. All around him were papers and files. The desk was covered with them, some had fallen to the floor, and he clutched one letter in his hand.

'Can you read what it says?' asked Lydia.

'Yes, it's from a building society warning him that

because he's in arrears with his mortgage, his apartment may be repossessed.'

Lydia nodded. 'He's over five months in arrears and owes the building society over £10,000. They're going to court to take the apartment from him.'

'£10,000! In five months! That's a mortgage of £2,000 a month!'

'Well, he borrowed over £400,000.'

'But why did they lend it to him if he couldn't afford to pay it back?'

'Because in some ways they didn't care whether he could or couldn't.'

Amy's head was whirling. Here was a man in a luxury apartment, filled with expensive furniture, who couldn't even repay his mortgage, and a building society that didn't care whether he did or didn't. 'Are you sure you got rid of all my paracetamol? I think I've got a headache coming on.'

Lydia smiled as she led Amy back on to the balcony and they gazed out across the water. 'One of the most basic principles of banking is that the bank is meant to "know its customer". Another is that of "responsible lending" – making sure that reasonable repayment can be managed without the customer having to sell their house or other property, or in extreme cases, trying to ensure that the debt will not lead to bankruptcy.

'When I was young, getting a mortgage out of a building society manager was like drawing teeth. You had to see them personally and then they grilled you as to whether you could afford to repay. At times it was almost as if they were lending you their own money. They would always write to your employers or, if you were self-employed, to your accountants, to make sure you earned what you said you did. When the whole process was over you were lucky if you managed to borrow two and half times your income.'

'What changed?'

'Well, in fairness to the lenders, quite a lot,' Lydia conceded. 'The concept of responsible lending is much more difficult to achieve when the customer has lots of credit from many different sources – store cards, credit cards, hire purchase, etc. Many lenders practically give up on "know your customer" and so fail in responsible lending. They often resort to relying on whatever information the borrower gives them and then they become obsessed not with your ability to repay, but with the simple matter of whether their money is safe. If it comes down to it they can get all they are owed by taking your house off you. In short, they forgot the personal relationship and became simply money lenders.'

Amy's headache was getting worse. 'So what went wrong for this man?'

'Well, from the building society's point of view, not much. He sold his last house before he bought this one, which meant he had a deposit of over £100,000. He paid just over half a million for the new apartment, so when the court orders it to be sold there will be plenty to pay the building society back all they lent him, plus their interest and all their costs in evicting him.'

'But why did they lend him the money in the first place if he didn't have the income to make the payments?' Amy persisted.

'Because they didn't ask about his income,' Lydia said. 'Well, that's not strictly true, but in this case they allowed him to "self-certify" his income – in other words, to tell them what he was earning without even checking with his employer.'

'And he made it up?'

'No, actually, in this case he didn't. He was just over-optimistic about the bonuses he thought he would be paid and the commissions he would earn. It wasn't quite fraudulent, but certainly a little Walter Mitty, and because of the downturn in financial markets his salary actually dropped a little. It only takes a 10 per cent drop in income to change manageable credit commitments into serious debt problems.'[1]

'But it's not too bad for him, is it?' Amy asked. 'I mean, he borrowed £400,000 and if the apartment is worth at least what he paid for it, he'll have plenty left, even after the building society have taken what they're owed.'

'If only that were so,' Lydia replied. 'Would you turn on the television, please.'

PROVING WHAT YOU'RE WORTH

Morning television was in full swing and a studio audience was discussing whether a life sentence really should be for life. Amy couldn't see the relevance to the man in despair in the room next door, but suddenly the debating stopped and the programme went to a commercial break.

'Watch carefully,' said Lydia, 'and note every word.'

Amy had seen the commercial dozens of times. A well-dressed, smiling, middle-aged man who somehow looked like everybody's father was telling the world about a company that would lend money without any 'hassle' or 'reams of paperwork'. In fact, the cheque could be in your account within forty-eight hours. You could use the money for any purpose – a car, a holiday, or 'that kitchen you've always dreamed of'. The commercial went on to show three couples who sang the praises of the company in terms of ease of the loan, minimum of formality, and sheer niceness. It closed with a cheque flying through the air and into somebody's account.

Lydia leaned forward and turned the television off. 'Did you notice anything strange?'

'Well, they said it was no problem if you had a bad repayment record, had difficulty in proving your income, and even if you had county court judgments registered against you. No money lender in the history of the world has ever said that!'

Lydia smiled. 'You're getting the hang of this, Amy. But what else did you see?'

Amy frowned. 'Only something about being a home owner.'

'You've got it in one! The exact words at the bottom of the screen were, "*Applicants must be over eighteen and be home owners*".'

'So, that's why they're prepared to take almost anybody. It's what we've just been talking about – so long as the lender knows there's enough value in the house, they don't much care whether you repay them properly or not. They'll get their money by selling your house.'

'That's about it,' Lydia agreed. 'In this case our man has given the finance company what's called a second mortgage.'

'So he has another mortgage on top of the building society one?'

'I'm afraid so – and at a much higher interest rate. He had lots of credit card debt and saw an advert that offered him the opportunity to roll all his borrowing into "one easy monthly payment".'

'But all this stuff!' said Amy, waving her hand around the apartment. 'He's so wealthy.'

'No, Amy, he's poor. In fact, he's poorer than some of the people on the other side of the road. Almost all of this "stuff", as you call it, has been bought on borrowed money – store cards, credit cards, even the holidays that lay behind those pictures on the wall – all borrowed money.'

'But he seems to have a good job.'

'He does have a good job. In fact he's a stockbroker.'

'You're joking!'

'No, I'm not. He earns in excess of £70,000 a year. But he spends every penny and a lot more.'

'But his job – I mean, doesn't he know what's happening?'

'Debt isn't logical, Amy, because often it isn't just about money. Such people often mix in circles where everybody wears expensive clothes, drives expensive cars and goes on expensive holidays. The only problem is that many of these people are not wealthy at all – but they earn just enough money to borrow enough to buy enough to fool each other enough. They may talk very grandly, but there is not much behind the façade. It's like the man at the party who said to a friend, "I've got the chance of a really great deal. I can buy a piece of land for a million pounds, get planning consent, spend another million developing it, and sell the whole project on, making a profit of two million. The only slight problem is that I need a £50 deposit."

'It reminds me of the story of the earthling and the alien:

The Alien and the Earthling

An alien and an earthling were hovering above the M25 motorway and watching the passing cars. The alien was trying to understand how dwellers of the tiny planet conducted their affairs. 'What are these two cars directly beneath us?' he asked.

'One is called a Lamborghini and the other a Mondeo,' replied the earthling.

'I can see that one is very cramped, in fact

the child in the back seat looks as if he is dying for lack of air, but the one you call a Mondeo has four large seats and lots of room. It's easy to see that the Lamborghini must be for your poorer people.'

The earthling laughed out loud. 'No – the Lamborghini is seven times as expensive as the Mondeo!'

The alien looked puzzled. 'That must be because the running costs are much less expensive.'

The earthling was beside himself at the alien's naivety. 'No – they're four times greater than on the Mondeo.'

'Will it hold its value better than the Mondeo?'

'No, it will drop in value in the first year to a sum equal to the total cost of the Mondeo!'

'How do most people pay for the Lamborghini?'

'They go to a money lender – we call them

finance companies – and they pay the money lender interest every month.'

'So these are not wealthy people?'

'Well, they're not short of a bob or two, but no, most of them don't have enough cash to buy a Lamborghini.'

'Why would anybody who can't really afford it pay all that interest to have the cramped car when they could have the one with all the room in it?'

The earthling was enjoying explaining things to his slower visitor. 'For two reasons. First the Lamborghini does almost 200 miles an hour!'

Even the alien was impressed – that was equal to one of their smaller inter-galactic run-abouts. 'Wow! Does the driver ever go that fast in it?'

'Oh no, by law he can only go seventy miles an hour – the same as the Mondeo driver – if he kept breaking the speed limit he'd be put in prison!'

> *The alien was totally confused but eager to learn. 'You said there were two reasons.'*
>
> *'Well, the second is that only very successful people can afford to own the Lamborghini; when you drive one of these other people know that you are clever.'*
>
> *It was the alien's turn to smile. 'Now I can see why humans have been so concerned to find intelligent life on other planets.'*

'It's not rocket science, Amy. If you can afford a Lamborghini all well and good, but if you've got one at the same time as you've got store card debt, credit card debt and a second mortgage that keeps you awake at night, or if you have to work such long hours to pay for the thing that you don't have time to spit, let alone smell the roses, then get a Mondeo! And this isn't just true for our wealthy pauper; sheer vanity and pride, and the desire to impress, can lead any of us into debt – whatever our income. Quentin Crisp put it well: "Never keep up with the Joneses. Drag them down to your level. It's cheaper." Anyway, our man hasn't got a Lamborghini but he does have something rather smart. Let's go down to the car park and have a look at it.'

THE COST OF SUCCESS

The undercroft parking lot was filled with impressive motors, but even so the brand-new sports car stood out.

'Well, what do you think of it?' said Lydia.

'It's gorgeous.'

'It certainly is: it cost over £30,000.'

'But he can't afford a car like that!'

'Amy, people get into debt for many reasons. This man has done so mainly in an effort to show that he's successful, and actually the vast majority of very expensive cars are bought on credit. Sometimes those interest rates are low and sometimes not, sometimes tax relief is available and sometimes not, but it's still credit and it still costs. And, anyway, he fell for the "what will it cost me monthly?" trick.'

'That sounds familiar.'

'Retailers love it – especially on high-value items like cars. They ask questions like, "How much did you plan to spend per month?" and, hey presto, a car doesn't cost £30,000, it costs £599 a month for five years. Our man juggled his monthly figures until he persuaded himself that he could afford it. If you can afford a fancy car, good luck to you, but don't mortgage your future for the sake of what is essentially a way to get from A to B. The only other thing you borrow a lot of money for is a house, but at least with that you've got a very good chance that it will appreciate over the years. A new car, though, devalues the second you register it. It's silly to borrow large sums to buy something that's likely to plummet in value. But that's not the worst part for him. Take a good look at his car. What do you think is its most expensive accessory?'

Amy wandered around the car. It had alloy wheels, a navigation system, and a stereo you'd be proud to have in your home. She had no idea which of these cost the most. Lydia pointed downwards. 'It's the number plate. Look – it's made up of his initials. It cost him over £20,000. Now how's that headache of yours, because it's time for a little maths.'

'I can manage,' said Amy, with her head pounding.

'The wealthy pauper upstairs has at least £20,000 of store card debt. He used the card for the furniture, the white goods in the kitchen, and most of his clothes. At the rates they charge he pays interest of £6,000 a year. To pay that after tax and national insurance he has to earn about £10,000 a year!'[2]

Amy was doing her best to keep up as Lydia gained speed. 'If he sold the personal number plate and re-registered his car with an ordinary number he could pay all the store cards off.'

Amy nodded as Lydia checked that she was keeping up. 'Do you see it, Amy? Over 10 per cent of this man's salary is going towards funding his number plate!'

'Then why doesn't he just sell it?'

Lydia paused. 'Now we're getting to the heart of why people with relatively high incomes can so easily get into debt. What does that number plate say about the driver?'

'That he's successful.'

'Well, that's the sad part. And you know, Amy, in many ways our man upstairs has known wonderful success. He has qualified in a very demanding profession, he's good at his job and he has great prospects. But he's trying to convince the world that he's more successful than he actually is. There's nothing wrong with a personalised number plate if you can afford it, but when we use things – cars, houses, clothes, any possession – to prove that we've "made it", we're normally in for a pretty unfulfilling life – because there will usually be somebody with more than us who will laugh at our trinkets. This man has dreamt most of his young life about earning the kind of income that he now enjoys, but it didn't matter how much he earned because he never learnt the money secret.'

'I didn't get into debt to prove I was successful,' Amy protested.

'No, my dear, you didn't. But many of us do spend money to somehow make ourselves feel special. Sometimes we even give expensive presents to feel significant – as if we matter. It's the biggest lesson of today: *I don't need to prove my worth by what I own.*' Lydia turned towards the door. 'Now it really is time for us to be leaving.'

'But what about the man upstairs? He seemed to be in despair.'

'Actually, he's not. In fact, all he can think about is preserving his image. He has a while to go before he's really ready to be free of debt.'

'But they're going to take his house.'

'Well, maybe not,' Lydia said. 'I hope he can swallow his pride and go to see somebody like Chloe – she won't be surprised to see somebody with a high income.'

'What can be done?'

'Quite a lot, actually. I'll put some notes about it in the biscuit tin for you.'

'You said a moment ago that he was in such trouble because he never learned the secret. Are we near to finding it now?'

'Very near indeed,' Lydia answered.

11
The Last Day

The two women left the apartment block and ambled along the waterfront. Amy was tired – it had been a long and emotionally draining day – and yet she felt exhilarated. She looked at the woman walking alongside her and suddenly thought that Lydia looked frail. The inner strength was still there but the spring in her step was gone. Amy hardly knew her but felt as if the older woman was almost like a mother to her. She thought about what Lydia had just said about the secret and realised that their time together was soon to be over.

She touched Lydia's arm. 'You saved my life.' Lydia smiled at her and Amy went on, 'It costs you to do this, doesn't it? I don't mean in money, but it costs you something inside, doesn't it?'

'Amy, there is so much pain in the world, and so many who live in the middle of a crowd are lonely. When I found you, your loneliness was greater than your debt.'

'But I had lots of people I could have spoken to – my friends or my parents.'

'Yes, you did, but for some reason you felt you couldn't. Perhaps it was because you felt a failure – as if you, alone in the whole world, were going through this dreadful experience. But I didn't threaten you, did I? I was old, and slightly dotty, and drank too much tea. It was easier for me to come to you.'

'But you still haven't answered my question.'

'What was it again?'

'About it costing you – you know – to do this.'

'Oh, Amy, I do this once in a while, but the real heroes are those who do it day in and day out in Citizens Advice Bureaux, debt counselling centres and credit unions all across the country.'

'But *you* did it for *me*.'

'Yes, I did. Now, enough of all that, it's time to discover the secret. I want to tell you about a man I came across some time ago who is quite fascinating – he developed the modern credit card.'

'I wouldn't have thought he was someone who would have been your hero!'

'Well, neither would I, but he is quite extraordinary. His name is Dee Hock.'

'Hock! You're joking!'

'No, I'm quite serious – he says it's one reason he never put his name on his own invention. In his words, "Who would want a credit card called Hock?"'

'When did he invent it?'

'Oh, in the late Sixties. Until he came along, credit card ownership was pretty exclusive but he developed a system of electrons and photons that bounced money around the universe and made credit cards available to the whole world. And he called it Visa International.'

'He must be a billionaire!'

'You'd think so. Visa does over $3 trillion – that's a thousand billion – dollars of business *every year*. If he'd taken just 0.5 per cent interest in the profits he would be richer than Bill Gates by a mile, but he never made much money out of the card itself. He really just wanted to prove to the financial world that it could be done.'

'When he sees the problem of debt, does he regret his invention?'

'Well, he believes that credit cards have brought much good – he says that e-commerce, for example, could never have developed without them – but in some ways he sees it as as much a failure as a success. He puts it like this, "Everything that has a power for good has equal power for evil." '[1]

'I bet he knows all the tricks to get the best out of his own credit cards.'

'Oh, he doesn't have any.'

'What!'

'Yes, he got rid of all his credit cards years ago.'

'But, why – if he invented them?'

'You can read "why" yourself,' said Lydia handing Amy a note. 'Somebody asked him the same question and the answer he gave was born out of an event long before he ever thought of Visa. In fact he was in his early thirties and had been laid off by a bank he'd worked for. I thought his words were so powerful that I wrote them down.'

I had no wish to be in debt. I took a lousy job, had three children to support and a small loan to service. I worked for a couple of years in jobs I hated, paying interest to get rid of that loan. After that I vowed I would never again be in more debt than I had cash in the bank. And I never have been.[2]

Amy looked up from the paper as Lydia continued. 'And then, Amy, the man who invented the Visa card, quoted something I want you never to forget:

Annual income £20, annual expenditure £19 19s 6d, result happiness; annual income £20, annual expenditure £20 0s 6d, result misery.[3]

'Dee Hock said, "There's still a lot to be said for that," and I agree with him. In fact, Amy, that's what it all comes down to. If you earn £1 but regularly spend

£1.10, there is no way back from debt. That works for individuals, for companies, for governments. In the long haul it always comes back to that.'

'That's the money secret, isn't it,' said Amy.

'Yes, it is. It doesn't matter how much you earn, how good your credit card rates are, how wonderful your computer programs are, or even how many debt books you read – there is only one way to be back in the black for ever.'

Amy was quiet for a long time. 'The strange thing, Lydia, is that everybody knows the secret. It's common sense really. We just forgot it.'

'But you know it now – not just in your head, but in your heart. And you've learnt it through pain – and pain is sometimes a very effective mentor.'

'Is that how you learned all of this – the hard way?'

'You will never know how hard. But enough of me. Will you make me two promises?'

'Anything.'

'I think it will take you two to three years to turn your finances around, and when you do, you will have at least £200 spare a month. When that happens

I want you to really go on the offensive against debt. In fact, I want you to knock it silly. And the place to begin is with your mortgage of £100,000. As soon as you can I want you to increase the monthly payment by £75 a month – just £17.31 a week. It will reduce your mortgage term by five whole years and save you over £20,000 in total.'[4]

'But that's staggering!'

'It is, and it's because of the sheer power of compound interest – which for most of your life has been working against you. It's why, if you only make the minimum monthly payment on a credit card, there is no way back from debt. But now it's going to work in your favour. Compound interest will become your friend.'

'And what's the second promise?'

'Oh, I don't have the right to ask it really, but I'd like you to take what you've learned over these few days and get alongside somebody else who really wants to be free of debt for ever. It's not surprising there are so many people with debt problems; so few of us have ever been taught to manage money or even do simple budgeting.' And with that, Lydia reached into a large plastic bag. 'And by the way, it's time for your graduation.'

Lydia handed Amy the biscuit tin. 'In some way this old tin holds the wisdom of all our time together. Use it to help yourself and others.'

Amy took it. She couldn't believe she could feel emotional about a battered tin but her voice caught in her throat as she spoke. 'I don't think I'll be much help to anybody. I've got to get out of my own financial mess first.'

'I know you're just beginning, but as I told you yesterday, you're a fast learner! And when people are in trouble they need those who have cried a little – who've been through some of the things they're experiencing. I believe you can help many others find the money secret, and anyway, I'm getting on a bit now!'

'Well, you'll have to let me in on some of your travel secrets!'

Lydia smiled; and with the smile she was gone.

Amy found herself on the platform of a railway station. A young man sat on a bench with his head in his hands. People rushed past him as though he wasn't there. She watched him for a while and then she heard her own voice, hesitant at first, then rising above the noise of the rush-hour:

'My name is Amy . . .'

The
Biscuit Tin

Losing Financial Control

Symptoms to watch out for are:

- Not being sure whether the cashpoint machine is going to pay out or not.

- Not being at all sure what figure will be at the end of a bank statement.

- Always being overdrawn.

- Losing track of the direct debits or standing orders that are operating on your account.

- Losing cash around the house or finding odd bits of cash – even bank notes – in various pockets.

- Readily borrowing from and lending money to friends.

- Impulse buying.

- Instead of asking, 'What is the total cost?' asking, 'Can I afford the monthly repayment?'

- Making minimum payments each month on credit cards.

- Not knowing the rate of interest you are paying on credit cards, store cards and bank borrowings.

- Getting taken in by offers of finance that come through the post.

- Leaving payment of bills until the last possible moment – certainly until the 'red' bill and often not until threatened with legal action.

Going on the Financial Weighing Scales

1 Collect the information you need for a financial reality check – this will be things like bank and credit card statements, bills, details of direct debits and the like.

2 Open any mail that you've got lying unopened in a pile, making sure you have a waste-paper bin near. Rip the junk mail up as you go, but put bills, statements, letters from creditors and any court summons to one side.

3 Now write a list of all the people to whom you owe money. Use the pay THEM FIRST system to identify the priority debts and make a list of them and the non-priority debts.

Tax (council)   **F**ines
Hire purchase   **I**ncome tax
Electricity/gas*   **R**ent/mortgage
Maintenance/child support   **S**econd mortgage
                                     Television licence

* You can't have your water cut off for non-payment unless you are a business so water debt is not a priority debt.

A typical list might look like this:

PRIORITY DEBTS	
Electricity	£87
Gas	£67
Mortgage	£566
Council tax	£400
Hire purchase car	£7,900

NON-PRIORITY DEBTS	
Bank overdraft	£500
Bank loan	£789
MasterCard	£488
Visa	£566
American Express	£900
Next store card	£233
Dixons store card	£1,200
John Mills catalogue	£455
Hire purchase on hi-fi	£1,450

4 Fill in the 'Reality Check' form below to calculate your actual income and expenditure every week or month. Always start with 'Income' – that's the easy part – and then fill in the 'Spending' part of the form.

5 A free legal advice centre will help you decide what monthly offers of payment you can offer to

each of your creditors, and come to an agreement
with them. All kinds of people from all walks of life
use advice centres and you will be helped in a non-
judgmental way.

REALITY CHECK FORM

INCOME	
Type	Weekly/monthly £
Basic salary/wages	
Partner's basic salary/wages	
Guaranteed overtime	
Partner's guaranteed overtime	
Bonuses	
Partner's bonuses	
Pension	
Child benefit	
Income support	
Job seeker's allowance	
Tax credits	
Maintenance/child support	
Other benefits (1)	
(2)	
Other income (1)	
(2)	
Total	

REALITY CHECK FORM

CURRENT SPENDING/REDUCED SPENDING	
Type	Weekly/monthly £
Mortgage/rent	
Second mortgage	
Endowment	
Ground rent	
Building insurance	
Contents insurance	
Council tax	
Water rates	
Gas	
Electricity	
Coal/oil	
Telephone/mobile phone	
TV licence/TV subscriptions	
TV rental	
Fines	
Petrol	
Car tax	
Car insurance	
Car servicing/repairs	
Car loan	
Pension	
Life insurance	
Child care	

THE BISCUIT TIN

Type	Weekly/monthly £
Maintenance	
House repairs/decoration	
Charitable giving	
Regular savings	
Housekeeping (food and cleaning supplies)	
Prescriptions	
Launderette/dry cleaning	
Newspapers	
Cigarettes	
Clothes	
Hobbies/sports/toys	
Entertainment	
Meals out/takeaways	
Gambling/bingo	
Christmas/birthday presents	
Holidays	
Emergencies	
Travel to work/school	
School dinners/meals at work	
Other school expenses	
Pocket money	
Pets	
Other (1)	
(2)	
Total	

Paying Credit and Store Card Arrears

Use as much money as possible to get rid of your credit card debt and especially any store card debts! Go to a free debt advice centre and ask them to work out how much you can allocate to repaying these.

List your credit and store cards showing the rates of interest on each. It might look like this.

CARD	AMOUNT OUTSTANDING	RATE OF INTEREST
Card 1	£1,000	29.90%
Card 2	£ 600	28.90%
Card 3	£ 890	19.00%
Card 4	£ 680	18.00%
Card 5	£ 560	18.00%
Card 6	£ 660	17.00%

Remember we talked about hitting the most expensive first. Start to pay the minimum amount each month on each card, except for the most expensive one. You should throw all you've got left from your credit card budget at this one. And when that is paid off, move on to the next one. You'll be amazed how fast those bullies fall!

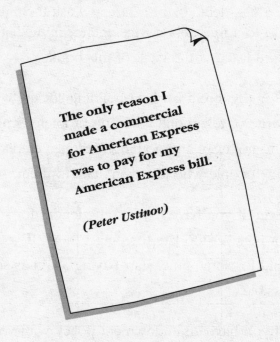

The only reason I made a commercial for American Express was to pay for my American Express bill.

(Peter Ustinov)

Remember the 'wealthy pauper' was in danger of losing his home – here are some ways to avoid that

1 Go to a free debt advice agency immediately – some are listed at the back of this book.

2 Don't ignore a bank or building society when they write or telephone you. The problem is not going to go away and nothing frustrates creditors as much as people who just won't talk to them.

3 Even if you have ignored the lender for some time, it is never too late to contact them. If you have not paid for some time, start paying again as soon as possible.

4 If you have an endowment policy with your mortgage, it may be a good idea to cash this in, but in some cases there may be a better option. Make sure you get independent advice.

5 If you have a repayment mortgage, ask the lender if they will allow you to pay interest only. This means that you won't actually be paying back any of the capital (the money you originally borrowed) and so your mortgage will take longer to repay, but it will give you a little breathing space. Your lender may insist that the 'interest only' arrangement is a temporary measure.

6 Ask the lender to roll your arrears into the amount you already owe and to extend the number of years over which you will be allowed to repay the mortgage. The advantage of this is that the arrears will be totally wiped off, but, of course, you will owe that extra sum and your mortgage will take longer to repay.

7 Ask the lender to allow you to make a reduced payment for a while. This is hard to get them to agree to, but they will sometimes do so because it is cheaper and easier for them than repossession proceedings.

8 Consider the possibility of whether you should sell your home and buy a less expensive one. Definitely do this before losing your home in repossession proceedings as you will almost certainly get a better price for it by selling it yourself.

9 Ask your local authority if they have a 'mortgage rescue scheme' for which you might qualify.

10 If court proceedings have already been issued, always attend the hearings. Remember that the court will want to keep you in your home if possible. Usually, if you show that you can make the normal monthly payments as well as repaying the arrears within a reasonable time, the court will suspend any possession order.

11 Don't be bullied into paying more than you can afford. Lenders often like the arrears to be cleared in one to two years, but if you cannot afford this, don't panic. Remember that it is up to the court, not the lender, what amount you should repay, and in some circumstances the court will allow you to stretch your repayment of the arrears over the remaining term of the mortgage.

⓬ Above all, don't put your head in the sand – get help as soon as possible.

Most banks and building societies don't want people to lose their homes. Just work with them – give them a chance to help you.

Frank and Sarah were considering bankruptcy. Here are a few notes ...

Dealing with Creditors – the Last Resort

There are several courses of action open to people which will allow them to pay their creditors what they can without having to deal with them directly. Bankruptcy is the most extreme, but in some cases is the most sensible route. Others are an Administration Order and an Individual Voluntary Arrangement. Here are some brief details, but if somebody is considering any of them they should get advice from a free advice centre.

Administration Order

If a person has debts of £5,000 or under, and at least one county court judgment, then it may be in their interest to apply for an Administration Order. They will need to complete an application form and take it to the court. If the Order is granted they will have to make one affordable monthly payment to the court who will distribute the money for them – the creditors can take no further action against them. After 3–5 years the court may order any outstanding balances to be written off.

Individual Voluntary Arrangement

This will allow a person to settle their debts without resorting to bankruptcy. It is a legally binding arrangement and is normally carried out with the help of a specialist insolvency expert who is usually a chartered accountant.

Under this agreement they will pay their creditors a lump sum or agreed instalments and in return the creditors will agree to write off part of the debt and not take court action against them or make them bankrupt. It only affects unsecured debts – so they will not be able to use this to deal with mortgage arrears on their home.

Bankruptcy

Bankruptcy can be a fresh start and a positive step. A person in debt can apply to a county court themselves to go bankrupt or, under certain circumstances, a creditor can apply. If it is a creditor, the application can be contested by the person in debt.

Many people considering bankruptcy are most worried about losing their home, but this is not inevitable. If the bankrupt owns his or her home, the trustee in bankruptcy will investigate whether it should be sold so that the equity (the money left after any mortgages are paid off) can be used to pay creditors.

If there is no equity, the trustee will often allow the bankrupt to keep the house and pay the mortgage – as long as the house is not excessively large. If the mortgage is very large the trustee could refuse to allow the bankrupt to keep sufficient income to pay the mortgage. It may be possible after a person is made bankrupt for a spouse or partner to buy the share of the property that is controlled by the trustee in bankruptcy. (Sometimes a sale can be arranged before going bankrupt.)

After the bankruptcy, creditors will not be able to pester the bankrupt person and will have to deal with the trustee in bankruptcy.

A bankruptcy is normally discharged after twelve months provided there is full co-operation with the trustee in bankruptcy. After the discharge, the former bankrupt is likely to find it difficult to obtain credit or get a mortgage for a number of years.

A decision to become bankrupt is a serious one and there are many issues which a free legal advice centre will be happy to discuss with you. It may have especially serious implications for those who own a property or business.

Some Golden Rules

1 Don't believe this is 'just me' – most people have known debt problems of some kind.

2 Don't feel you have to deal with the problem on your own. There are many free advice agencies, including the CAB, who are ready to help in a non-judgmental way.

3 Don't ignore the problem – perhaps by leaving letters unopened or refusing to speak to those to whom you owe money – it won't go away.

4 Don't go to debt management companies that offer to negotiate with your creditors in return for payment. They often offer to reduce your monthly repayments, but the way they deal with debt and the fees they charge often make things worse.

5 Always get in touch with your creditors and explain your difficulties.

6 Always keep copies of the letters you write and receive, and make notes of phone conversations.

7 Always attend court hearings. The county court is not one that deals with criminal matters, there is no jury.

8 Beware of borrowing even more money to clear off existing debts.

9 Be especially careful not to borrow any more money using your house as security – even if it means your total monthly repayments would be reduced – without getting advice from a free advice agency.

10 Try not to let worry over money overwhelm you. It is of great concern, but the most important thing in life is relationships. The hardest thing is to keep a sense of perspective. Don't battle on alone. With help, you will come through this difficult time.

References

1   The Wishing Well

1   *In Too Deep: CAB Clients' Experience of Debt*, Citizens Advice Bureaux, 2003.

2   *Financial Risk Outlook*, Financial Services Authority, 2003.

2   Know the Worst

1   'A Mintel survey has found that one in five gym members go just once a month or less' (*Guardian*, 28 October 2003).

3 Choose Your Weapons

1 YouGov survey carried out on behalf of KPMG, 2003.

2 Currys and Dixons have interest-free loan offers, with loans over four years at 29.5 per cent APR if the loans are not repaid within the interest-free periods (June 2004).

3 *Guardian*, 14 September 2002.

4 *The Dilbert Future*, Scott Adams, HarperCollins, 1997.

4 Retail Therapy

1 http://www.smh.com.au/articles/2003/08/17/1061059721181.html, 18 August 2003.

2 *Oxford Advanced Learner's Dictionary*, Oxford University Press, 2003.

3 *Ibid.*

4 Publicis study quoted in *Observer*, 6 May 2001.

5 *Ibid.*

6 http://www.coastnews.com/health/affluenza.html, 14 July 2004.

7 http://www.thestdavidshotel.com/offer_retail.html, 8 July 2004.

8   http://eshop.msn.com/columns.aspx?csID=59&page=0, 10 July 2004.

9   *Ibid.*

10 http://www.guardian.co.uk/Archive/Article/0,4273,4181822,00.html, 14 July 2004.

11 http://www.coastnews.com/health/affluenza/html, 14 July 2004.

5   First Things First

1   *Escape from Debt*, Keith Tondeur, Credit Action, 1993.

2   *Guardian*, 9 December 2003.

3   Imprisonment is only possible if the debtor has committed and is convicted of a criminal offence, i.e. fraud or theft. For instance, if a false name has been given in order to get a loan, then a prosecution may be brought. The Inland Revenue or Customs and Excise may prosecute for tax or VAT evasion. Finally, prosecution for bankruptcy offences is possible, though rare. A bankrupt's finances will be investigated by the Official Receiver to check there has been no fraud or any dishonest attempt to avoid paying creditors.

6   A House of Cards

1   Datamonitor, 2003.

2   Office of National Statistics, 2003.

3   *The European Credit Card Market*, Mintel, February 2004.

4   Frank O'Donnell, *The Scotsman*, 17 March 2004.

5   Tim Adams, *Observer*, 18 April 2004.

6   *Daily Telegraph*, 17 October 2003.

7   *Escape from Debt*, Keith Tondeur, Credit Action, 1993.

8   *Credit Card Survey*, Office of Fair Trading, March 2004.

9   NOP survey on behalf of Egg the Internet Bank, quoted in the *Sunday Times*, 23 March 2003.

10 'This is another example of consumers being duped by banks that are offering dazzling headline rates that often fail to sparkle' (*Sunday Times*, 30 May 2004).

11 This assumes that there is a monthly interest rate of 1.58 per cent, that only 3 per cent minimum is paid off, and that there are other debts on the card. Even after fifteen years, almost £1 out of the original £14.50 would still be outstanding.

12 'In many people's eyes, credit cards encouraged the growth in consumerism and consumer borrowing that occurred in the 1980s, but the greatest concern of all lies in the belief that they encouraged young people in particular to live far beyond their means, buying consumer goods they could ill afford' (*Paying with Plastic*, Karen Rowlingson and Elaine Kempson, Policy Studies Institute, 1994).

13 *Credit Card Survey*, Office of Fair Trading, March 2004.

14 *Over Indebtedness in Britain*, Elaine Kempson, DTI, 2002.

15 *Ibid.*

16 *Financial Mail on Sunday*, 11 January 2004.

17 'Money Talk', Stuart Cliffe, Chief Executive, National Society of Banking and Insurance Customers.

18 Debenhams card APR 28.0 per cent on purchases where repayments are made by direct debit, Frasercard APR 29.3 per cent on retail purchases, June 2004.

19 This assumes a monthly rate of 2.08 per cent

(APR 28.0 per cent), minimum repayments of 4 per cent and that there are other debts on the card. Even after fifteen years, almost £1 would still be owed.

20 Mintel Market report, May 2003, quoted in *Think Before You Borrow*, Office of Fair Trading, 2003.

21 http://news.bbc.co.uk/1/hi/business/3065919. STM (John McFall, Chairman, Treasury select committee, quoted by Andrew Verity, BBC Personal Finance Reporter, 14 July 2003).

8 Don't Trust Your Grandmother

1 Personal correspondence given to the author from a customer of one of the major banks.

2 Based on actual events that took place in April 2004 involving one of the major banks.

3 http://www.fool.co.uk/news/foolseyeview/2003/fev031218c.html (The Motley Fool, Cliff D'Arcy, 18 December 2003).

4 http://www.david-clelland.org.uk/030212poverty.html (David Clelland, MP, debate in the House of Commons on Low Income, Debt and Poverty, 12 February 2003).

9 Debt at the Door

1 *Over Indebtedness in Britain*, Elaine Kempson, DTI, 2002.

2 Felicity Lawrence, *Guardian*, 2 December 2002.

3 Calculated using TRURATE Plus © Brian Stewart Version 3:1.

4 *Ibid.*

5 *Ibid.*

6 Justin Harper, *Daily Mail*, 25 September 2003.

7 *Over Indebtedness in Britain*, Elaine Kempson, DTI, 2002.

8 Libby Purves, *The Times*, September 2003.

9 *Hard Work*, Polly Toynbee, Bloomsbury, 2003.

10 Calculated using TRURATE Plus © Brian Stewart Version 3:1.

11 'According to the New Economics Foundation, the nation's poorest households are at the mercy of a cabal of moneylenders, cheque cashers and dubious secondary mortgage lenders, charging interest rates of between 60% and 200%, and collecting a tidy £17bn between them. Britain, unlike other G7 nations that place a ceiling on interest rates, looks the other way while such

remorseless profiting from poverty takes place' (Rachel Shabi, *Guardian*, 17 April 2004, referring to *Profiting from Poverty – Why Debt is Big Business in Britain*, Henry Palmer and Pat Conaty, NEF Pocketbook 8, 2002).

10 The Wealthy Pauper

1   CAB Survey 2002 quoted in *Life After Debt*, Alex Keen, Which? Books, 2003.

2   To earn £6,000 net, the wealthy pauper, who is a higher-rate tax payer, must earn £10,169, paying £4,067 income tax and £102 national insurance.

11 The Last Day

1   Tim Adams, *Observer*, 18 April 2004.

2   *Ibid.*

3   'Annual income twenty pounds, annual expenditure, nineteen, nineteen and six, result happiness. Annual income twenty pounds, annual expenditure twenty pounds ought and six, result misery' (*David Copperfield*, Charles Dickens, Bradbury and Evans, 1849–50).

4   Mortgage of £100,000 at 6 per cent over twenty-five years is £652 per month, with the total amount repaid being £195,600 (using mortgage repayment tables issued by the Council of Mortgage Lenders).

i.   If you increase payments to £727 per month (an increase of £17.31 per week), the total repaid is reduced to £174,400 (a reduction of £21,200) and it reduces the mortgage period by five years.

ii. If you increase payments to £858 per month (an increase of £47.54 per week), you save £41,100 and reduce the mortgage period by ten years.

Useful Contacts

SOURCES OF INDEPENDENT DEBT ADVICE

Citizens Advice Bureaux
Tel: phone number listed in telephone directory.
www.adviceguide.org.uk

Consumer Credit Counselling Service (CCCS),
Wade House, Merrion Centre, Leeds, LS3 8NG
Tel: 0800 138 1111
www.cccs.co.uk

Credit Action, Howard House, The Point, Weaver Road, Lincoln, LN6 3QN
Tel: 01522 699777
www.creditaction.org.uk

National Debtline, The Arch, 48–52 Floodgate Street, Birmingham, B5 5SL
Tel: 0808 808 4000
www.nationaldebtline.co.uk

NATIONAL ASSOCIATIONS

Contact these to get details of local advice centres

AdviceUK (Federation of Independent Advice Centres – FIAC), 12th Floor, New London Bridge House, 25 London Bridge Street, London, SE1 9ST
Tel: 020 7407 4070
www.adviceuk.org.uk

Money Advice Scotland, Suite 306, Pentagon Centre, 36 Washington Street, Glasgow, G3 8AZ
Tel: 0141 572 0427
www.moneyadvicescotland.org.uk

National Consumer Council, 20 Grosvenor Gardens, London, SW1W 0DH
Tel: 020 7730 3469
www.ncc.org.uk

OTHER SOURCES OF ADVICE

Inland Revenue Self-Assessment Helpline
Tel: 0845 9000 444

Insolvency Service Central Enquiry Line, 21 Bloomsbury Street, London, WC1B 3QW
Tel: 020 7291 6895

ETHICAL LENDERS

Association of British Credit Unions, Holyoake House, Hanover Street, Manchester, M60 0AS
Tel: 0161 832 3694
www.abcul.org or www.creditunioncommunities.org

REGULATORS

Financial Services Authority (FSA), 25 The North Colonnade, Canary Wharf, London, E1 5HS
Consumer Helpline: 0845 606 1234
www.fsa.gov.uk

Office of Fair Trading (OFT), Fleetbank House, 2–6 Salisbury Square, London, EC4Y 8JX
Tel: 0845 722 4499
www.oft.gov.uk

Office of Gas and Electricity Markets (OFGEM), 9 Millbank, London, SW1P 3GE
Tel: 0845 906 0708
www.ofgem.gov.uk

Office of Telecommunications Ombudsman Service (OTELO), PO Box 730, Warrington, WA4 6WU
Tel: 0845 050 1614
www.otelo.org.uk

Trading Standards – phone number listed in telephone directory (possibly under name of local council)

www.consumercomplaints.org.uk

TV Licensing (General Enquiries) Bristol BS98 1TL

Tel: 0870 241 6468

www.tvlicensing.co.uk

Water Voice – there are ten regional offices in England and Wales – see telephone directory

www.ofwat.gov.uk

For further information visit:

www.themoneysecret.info